Praise for *Brand Now*

"A masterpiece of practical advice. This is the real-world playbook we've been waiting for."
—**MARK SCHAEFER**, author of *The Content Code* and *Known*

"Whether you're running a startup or a Fortune 500 company, your brand is often your most valuable asset. Yet breaking through is harder than ever in this noisy, distracted world. Nick Westergaard shows you exactly how to establish the reputation you want, for your company or yourself."
—**DORIE CLARK**, author of *Stand Out* and *Reinventing You*, and adjunct professor at Duke University's Fuqua School of Business

"*Brand Now* is an effective guide for building a brand regardless of size, while incorporating a formula for standing out in a competitive and distracted digital world."
—**STEVE LACROIX**, Executive Vice President & Chief Marketing Officer, Minnesota Vikings

"In today's raucous digital environment, it is increasingly difficult for brands to stand out and remain relevant. In *Brand Now*, Nick Westergaard offers a sensible framework and practical set of tools to help marketers build brands that move from person to person, platform to platform, and community to community."
—**ANDY CUNNINGHAM**, author of *Get to Aha!*, founder and CEO of Cunningham Collective, member of Apple's original Macintosh launch team

"Most people think of logos and colors when considering brand. But Nick shows us there are so many more building blocks that contribute to our customers' sense of our brand: online, offline, music, even scent. In an engaging style, he helps you choose the right branding tools so you align with your marketplace and grow your business."
—**DAVID MEERMAN SCOTT**, marketing strategist, entrepreneur, and bestselling author of ten books, including *The New Rules of Marketing and PR*

"With *Brand Now*, Westergaard provides the systematic approach that every modern brand builder needs to stand out in our distracted, digital world." **—JEFF ROSENBLUM,** author of *Friction* and director of *The Naked Brand*

"Nick Westergaard has always been quick to break down the essential touchpoints in marketing and branding. In *Brand Now*, he takes us through what it means to be a brand today—then provides actionable ways to align your brand with today's moments and experiences. This book works at both the top and bottom of the sales funnel." **—PATRICK HANLON,** author of *Primal Branding* and *The Social Code*

"Wow! Nick's kickass advice on brand-building is spot on. I found my head shaking an emphatic 'Yes!' as I read through each easily digestible nugget of advice." **—SUZY BATIZ,** CEO and founder of Poo~Pourri, author of *The Woo of Poo*

"*Brand Now* is the blueprint every business leader needs for building a brand in today's complex, cluttered, and competitive environment. It's an immensely practical and easy-to-read resource that I highly recommend." **—DENISE LEE YOHN,** author of *What Great Brands Do* and *Fusion*

"A surprising few have tackled the task of redefining what it means to build a brand in a digitally driven age and Westergaard has done it like no one else. *Brand Now* is not an intellectual exercise; it's a straightforward guide for marketers big and small." **—ANDREW M. DAVIS,** bestselling author of *Brandscaping* and *Town Inc.*

"The concept of branding is, perhaps, one of the most confusing and misunderstood practices in marketing strategy. In *Brand Now*, not only does Nick demystify the art and science of branding, and set us all straight; he does so while simultaneously clearing the road for the new, modern brand strategy. *Brand Now* is, quite simply, the twenty-first century guidebook every marketer needs." **—ROBERT ROSE,** author of *Killing Marketing*, Chief Strategy Officer, The Content Advisory

"It doesn't matter if you are with a multinational conglomerate or a one-person shop in a garage—guess what? You've got a brand. Nick has given us a very practical primer on the components of a brand, and a handy toolbox of resources any brand can make use of. A brand is the sum total of each interaction between company and customer—and Nick's process will help you maximize every one of those interactions to create a compelling, lasting brand that stands for something." **—TOM WEBSTER**, Vice President, Strategy and Marketing, Edison Research

"For years, I've believed the future of business is marketing with people and not at them. That future is here and so is your roadmap on how to navigate branding today. *Brand Now* is the perfect guide to telling your story and connecting with people in a meaningful way." **—JOHN MICHAEL MORGAN**, author of *Brand Against the Machine*

"A good majority of business books aren't terribly effective because there is a lot of navel gazing and theory thrown around without any practical experience. That's not the case with *Brand Now*. Nick Westergaard has made branding for any size business approachable and exciting. If you're just starting out or you have been in business for years, *Brand Now* will help you build a brand, both online and off." **—GINI DIETRICH**, founder and CEO of Arment Dietrich, and author of *Spin Sucks*

"Buying behavior has completely changed over the past 20 years. Unfortunately, most companies have not. *Brand Now* will help you catch up quickly . . . and guide you through the forest. It's both practical and fun. Enjoy!" **—JOE PULIZZI**, author of bestselling marketing books, including *Killing Marketing* and *Content Inc.*, and founder, Content Marketing Institute

"*Brand Now* shakes off your old views of what matters to a company's brand and gives you a framework and tools to work across the channels where you'll be seen and experienced. Get into this Nick Westergaard wizardry now and sharpen up that brand of yours." **—CHRIS BROGAN**, CEO, Owner Media Group

"You might take branding for granted—it's just there because it's always been there. Well, Nick reminds us that branding is difficult and is getting only more complex in the digital age. Lucky you—you're now holding the key to unlocking the future of branding."

—**SCOTT MONTY**, CEO, Brain+Trust Partners

"If there is one thing that every business or organization has in common, it's that we want to stand out. We want the world to notice us and ultimately trust us. And with this tremendous read by Nick Westergaard, your business, regardless of shape or size, can do just that. He gives the framework. He gives the exercises. It's all here. For anyone willing to do the work to truly build their brand in an ultra-distracted world, I highly recommend *Brand Now*."

—**MARCUS SHERIDAN**, author of *They Ask, You Answer*

"In this incredibly useful guide to building a brand in a constantly shifting landscape, Nick Westergaard takes the approach of focusing on frameworks rather than rigid rules. His book helps organizations of any size—from entrepreneurs to multinational companies—find stability and brand strength by concentrating on core principles that never change even as the technologies and channels do."

—**TAMSEN WEBSTER**, CEO and
Chief Message Strategist, The Red Thread

"We live in a world with a sub-three-second attention span. Want to matter? Want to be heard? Then your brand needs to be top of mind, all the time. How to make sure it is? Read this book."

—**PETER SHANKMAN**, author of *Faster Than Normal*

"For brands, digital changes everything—but 99 percent of marketing teams are still playing yesterday's game. With the *Brand Now* framework, Nick has written the definitive playbook for the way brands needs to be managed today."

—**DOUG KESSLER**, cofounder, Velocity Partners

BRAND NOW

HOW TO STAND OUT IN A CROWDED, DISTRACTED WORLD

NICK WESTERGAARD

with Illustrations by the Author

AMACOM

AMERICAN MANAGEMENT ASSOCIATION

New York • Atlanta • Brussels • Chicago • Mexico City • San Francisco
Shanghai • Tokyo • Toronto • Washington, D.C.

This publication is designed to provide accurate and authoritative information in regard to the subject matter covered. It is sold with the understanding that the publisher is not engaged in rendering legal, accounting, or other professional service. If legal advice or other expert assistance is required, the services of a competent professional person should be sought.

Library of Congress Cataloging-in-Publication Data

Names: Westergaard, Nick, author.
Title: Brand now : how to stand out in a crowded, distracted world / by Nick
    Westergaard ; with illustrations by the author.
Description: New York, NY : AMACOM, [2018] | Includes bibliographical
    references and index.
Identifiers: LCCN 2017051426 (print) | LCCN 2017054658 (ebook) | ISBN
    9780814439234 (ebook) | ISBN 9780814439227 (hardcover)
Subjects: LCSH: Branding (Marketing)
Classification: LCC HF5415.1255 (ebook) | LCC HF5415.1255 .W4157 2018 (print)
    DDC 658.8/27—dc23
LC record available at https://lccn.loc.gov/2017051426

About AMA
American Management Association (www.amanet.org) is a world leader in talent development, advancing the skills of individuals to drive business success. Our mission is to support the goals of individuals and organizations through a complete range of products and services, including classroom and virtual seminars, webcasts, webinars, podcasts, conferences, corporate and government solutions, business books, and research. AMA's approach to improving performance combines experiential learning—learning through doing—with opportunities for ongoing professional growth at every step of one's career journey.

10 9 8 7 6 5 4 3 2 1

To the standout brands—from Starbucks to Star Trek.
And to the stars of my life—Meghann,
Harry, Sam, Adrien, Mia, and Jude.

Contents

Introduction

My wife and I have five kids. This is an important detail, as it tells you who I am in a lot of ways. It means I know about bringing order out of chaos. It means I know about compromise and pleasing different constituencies with diverse and sometimes contradictory needs. It means I know about making resources stretch just a bit further. It also means I do a lot of shopping at Costco.

On a fall day a few years ago, I found myself avoiding a challenging project by escaping to Costco. I had just learned that I would be covering the spring branding courses for a colleague who was going on sabbatical. Having taught social media marketing at the University of Iowa since 2012, most of my curriculum has been focused on the forefront of digital marketing. With new platforms, features, and more, there's plenty to talk about. But what can you say about branding? It's important . . . It's been around forever . . . But . . . it's changing . . . Don't we need toilet paper? I'm pretty sure we do. I'd better go to Costco. . . .

Another by-product of having five kids? I'm rarely alone. I'm carrying my then two-and-a-half-year-old son Jude as I walk through the massive enclosed warehouse that is our Costco's parking structure. I place him in the standard-issue Costco cart, which is roughly the size of a Ford Focus. I only needed a couple of things, so naturally I filled the entire cart.

A trip to Costco is one of the easier errands to run with kids. As the store is so big, they probably won't mow down too many innocent bystanders. Plus, everything's in huge boxes ensconced in thick metal shelving, meaning they won't take down an end-cap of glass jars of pasta sauce. There are also free samples of food. It's not always exciting food from a kid's perspective (chocolate-covered kale chips?), but it meets the most important criterion: it's in front of them and free.

At two years and change, my son isn't exactly a toddling ency-clopedia. He also has his mouth stuffed full of Skinny Pop. So, I'm extra-surprised when, while walking past an aisle, he says, "Coffee!" I stop. As a sleep-deprived parent, my first response is "Where?" Then I'm more curious. We were passing an aisle. I wasn't even looking for coffee (I mean, I'm *always* looking for coffee; but you get my point). I scanned the horizon and ventured nearly halfway down the aisle, where we walk past the Keurig K-Cups (available at Costco in refrigerator-sized boxes). We go past Green Mountain, Newman's Own, and Kirkland. As we creep up on the Starbucks brand, Jude once again says "Coffee!"

Then I start to put it all together. Jude tags along with us every-where, as he's the youngest. To parent the aforementioned kids, my wife and I consume in coffee what would be comparable to what a zoo keeps on hand to feed an elephant. The Starbucks drive-thru is a favorite stop. "Hang on a sec, Mom and Dad have to get some coffee," we say as we pass the big sign with the mermaid. That's why he responded to the Starbucks box in the store. It had the mermaid on it. She means coffee. She *is* coffee.

All of a sudden, a toddler has been imprinted by a massive cate-gory leader. The world is a distracting place. For both toddlers and grown-ups. It's hard to make sense of it all. To do so, we look for patterns and assign meanings. This is a car. That is a dog. The mer-maid sign is coffee.

And that's how a trip to Costco focused my thinking on how we brand now. To build standout brands in today's distracted digital world, we need to remember that most of us have the attention span of a toddler as we are presented with an overwhelming amount of stimuli. We need to create and reinforce easily recognizable patterns. We need to create meaning. This is challenging when few understand branding itself.

When I was a guest on his podcast, success coach and speaker Mitch Matthews introduced me as "the Indiana Jones of branding and marketing." Not because of my beard stubble and roguish charm, but because I split my time between the college classroom and the corporate conference room. I consult with organizations big and small. From small businesses and start-ups to Fortune 500 companies. From nonprofit organizations to President Obama's Jobs Council. And I can tell you that everyone has their own definition of branding.

How did we get here?

Cows to Computers: A Brief History of Branding

One of the most quoted lines in Edward Albee's one-act play *The Zoo Story* states that "sometimes a person has to go a very long distance out of his way to come back a short distance correctly."[1] To chart the best path ahead in our confusing media landscape, we have to start with a primer on the history of branding. The word *brand* comes from the Dutch word . . . *brand*. It means "to burn" and came to prominence as the Dutch East India Company burned its mark onto its products. When asked what images you associate with branding, I bet most would still cite the iron used in cattle branding.

Historically, we've been less subtle with our branding. Instead of carefully communicating a set of messages over time, our predecessors just got an iron with our symbol hot and burned it into the thing that we wanted to mark. From Roman glassblowers to nineteenth-century cattle ranchers. How easy would it have been to be in charge of branding back then? *Heat the iron, heat the iron, heat the iron, heat the iron. SSSSCCHHHHH! Mooooo! Done. Next.*

What happened after that? Brand consultancy Interbrand, famous for its first-of-a-kind ISO-certified Best Global Brands report examining the world's 100 most valuable brands, has identified what they call the four ages of branding.[2] And, yes, the first stage is the cow-burning thing.

That's because this first stage is defined by identity. The need to differentiate your products and services from your competitors. What started as a means of sorting cattle grew with the industrial revolution to help communicate to consumers which products they should buy. What's unique? What's different about this product versus that one? Why is Coca-Cola better than Pepsi? Names, logos, slogans, and mascots were the tools of the trade that got the job done. This era continued for most of the twentieth century.

During the financial heyday of the 1980s, organizational assets were more closely examined in terms of their value. As marketing costs became brand investments, the second age of branding—the age of value—was born. This heightened awareness of brand value also led to a bigger-picture view of branding. Maybe your brand wasn't just what your advertisements said. Maybe your brand was made up of the service that customers received in your store. This led to a more sophisticated approach to brand management. As IBM expanded their business beyond mainframe computing, it became important to communicate the value of the IBM brand in new product and service extensions such as consulting.

With the Internet came more advanced tools for crafting meaningful experiences. Information gained online guided customers in-store, where they looked for a seamless brand experience. A better integration of what we were saying online and what we were doing offline, in-store. This third age of branding was the age of experience. Steve Jobs turned heads when he returned to Apple and promptly announced a new focus on retail stores. "Why would you go to an Apple Store?" many thought at the time. Today, can you imagine *not* going to an Apple store? It wouldn't be the same brand experience without it.

Finally, with increased social and mobile technology, organizations are able to mine our data and craft a unique, personalized experience based on you, the consumer. This is the age of *you*. Uber creates a ride where you need one. Your Amazon home page looks different than mine. And they look different when we're on our phones versus our desktops.

Branding is more important now than ever. According to the latest edition of the biennial Chief Marketing Officer (CMO) Survey from Duke University's Fuqua School of Business, CMOs expect to be allocating more and more of their budgets to brand-building, an increase of 4.3 to 6.3 percent from just two years ago.[3] This increase puts branding on par with the increases projected for other, more frequently cited marketing expenditures such as customer relationship management (CRM) tools and marketing research and intelligence.

In digging deeper, these bullish increases are tied to an enhanced perception of brand value among marketers. The CMO Survey reports a 3.8 percent increase in the importance of brand value, up from 3.3 percent the previous year.[4] This puts growth in brand value ahead of the growth rates for other customer metrics such as acquisition and retention. It's also worth noting that brand awareness and brand-building are among the most popular uses of social media, whose budget allocation continues to grow as well.

We've come a long way from burning things. But the history is key. In the past, we branded things. It was something that we did— sometimes with a hot iron, sometimes with a TV commercial—to someone else. It was kind of simple. Today, we live in a noisy, wonderful, crazy, distracting interconnected and increasingly digital world. Brands are the patterns we can use to make sense of it all and communicate what we have and what we're doing for others.

In a crowded, complex world, your brand has to stand out.

Branding and the Scrappy Hobbits

In 2014, I was where I am right now. Writing what would become my first book, *Get Scrappy: Smarter Digital Marketing for Businesses Big and Small*. I had a prescriptive plan for how one would get scrappy with their digital marketing. You'd start with the smart steps you can't skip—your strategy. From there, you embrace key tactics to help you do more with less and then, finally, simplify your efforts for the long haul. Before you can do anything with digital media, you have to make sure you have a solid brand. So, I started writing the first chapter focused on the basics of brand-building. Like all things in *Get Scrappy*, I was aiming for a short, concise chapter.

At 7,000-plus words, there was no end in sight. When I showed an early draft to Ann Handley, best-selling author of *Everybody Writes*, she noted: "You . . . have a lot of stuff on branding there at the beginning." One of these chapters was not like the others. I set the bloated branding chapter aside and rewrote it as a scrappy brand blueprint. A quick-start guide to branding. That was the first moment when I felt like the chapter I'd started could be another book.

It reminded me of the story of J.R.R. Tolkien and the genesis of *The Lord of the Rings* trilogy. It started with a simple charge: write a sequel to *The Hobbit*. Like my branding chapter, his sequel escalated as quickly as a Ron Burgundy street fight. However, unlike Professor Tolkien, I've managed to spare you from an epic high-fantasy trilogy of branding books.

Instead, I want to take the bones of what I started in that chapter, and combine them with what I ended up exploring in my University of Iowa branding classes, thanks to a trip to Costco and a reminder about patterns and meaning. I'll also draw on my consulting work and my experience as host of the *On Brand* podcast, where I talk with brand-builders at organizations like Adobe, Allianz, Ben & Jerry's, Cisco, McDonald's, the Minnesota Vikings, Salesforce, and *The Onion*. These interviews left patterns of their own, showing what today's most memorable brands are doing to stand out.

To brand now, you have to both build and move your brand. "Where are these brands going?" you may ask. They must move between everyone, everywhere—both online and off. Why? Because a static brand just won't cut it. Word of mouth has always been the most compelling yet elusive marketing medium. And while digital distracts, it's also provided one of the greatest advances in word-of-mouth marketing. Previously if someone had a positive interaction with your brand—great service, an engaging TV spot—they would activate word-of-mouth momentum by telling a few people who in turn would tell a few more. Today, tools like Facebook, Instagram, and Snapchat have scaled word of mouth exponentially.

But the opportunity is squandered if we don't focus on building brands that move. Brands that move from person to person, platform to platform, and community to community. It's not enough to create a brand or rebrand your existing brand and simply hope that the rest of the world finds out about it. They won't. It's too noisy out there. To stand out, you need to build a brand that moves.

The Brand Now Framework

So how do you create movement? With dynamics. Merriam-Webster defines dynamics as "a branch of mechanics . . . that deals with forces and their relation primarily to the motion . . . of bodies."[5] Forces in motion. To build and move our brands, we need to understand the dynamics at play.

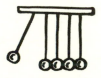

First, basic brand-building still matters. Your brand has to stand for something. It has to have meaning to stand out. From here, we need to look at the structures we use for building. The pieces that make up our brand DNA are more unique than in years past. What works for one brand may not work for you. Storytelling is one of the best tools for making sense of the world around us. Our brains are hardwired for stories. You need to embrace this and hone your brand's unique story. But this is certainly no guarantee that your brand will move, online or off.

That's where today's digital dynamics come into play. When you create content like blog posts, videos, and podcasts that help your customers, they'll be more compelled to share it. When you embrace the power of your online community of fans and followers—both internally and externally—you create a powerful ally. However, these relationships are fragile in today's transparent, noisy world, which is why clarity is important. Transparent, simple brands stand out and move faster.

Finally, experience continues to be a driver of brand loyalty. This is more than just being consistent: you need to create a coherent brand experience that your community can be a part of.

Part One of this book will focus on the seven Brand Now Dynamics, with a chapter for each:

1. Meaning
2. Structure
3. Story
4. Content
5. Community
6. Clarity
7. Experience

Throughout these chapters, we'll explore what each dynamic means and close with exercises and action items—"building blocks"—that you can use to get started.

It's not hard to get me monologuing about how everything is brand—small businesses, Fortune 500 companies, products, nonprofits, government agencies. And also personal brands, political brands, associations, and membership organizations. Everyone, to a certain extent, is a brand and/or a part of a brand several times over. I'm all kinds of fun at a cocktail party! While I include examples of many different types of brands throughout Part One of the book, I wanted to do more. There are also other key tactics and touchpoints important to the process that merit deeper dives. That's why Part Two is a Brand Now Toolbox featuring applications of the Brand Now Dynamics for specific types of brands and in specific situations, such as B2B branding and crisis communications.

Branding is more important now and more challenging now than ever before. Marketing and media change is constant, but your brand is an asset that never depreciates. That is, it never depreciates as long as you take care of it. As Deb Gabor, CEO of Sol Marketing, notes, "It's brand or be branded." Create your own story before someone else does it for you.[6]

We need to stand out. We need to grow. And we have more tools for doing so. The problem lies in the fact that consumers are bombarded with thousands of brand messages each day. It's not enough to simply do more. We have to do more of what works. More of what helps and less of what hinders.

Let's get moving. Let's brand now.

Dynamic (definition)

dy·nam·ic

dī'namik/

noun—a force that stimulates change or progress
within a system or process.

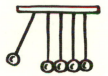

I

The Brand
NOW
Dynamics

ONE
Meaning

If you follow the winding cobblestone streets where hip downtown Seattle meets the bustling public market overlooking the Elliott Bay waterfront, past the fresh seafood, fruits, vegetables, specialty breads, artisan oils, handmade jewelry, street musicians, and salt-water taffy, you'll find a Starbucks.

As the joke goes, there's a Starbucks on every corner. In Seattle, that's pretty much true, as Starbucks has 23 coffee shops for every 100,000 residents, the most per-capita in the United States.[1] But the Starbucks I'm standing in front of at 1912 Pike Place is no ordinary Starbucks: it's the very first Starbucks. I interact with Starbucks at some level every day. From the coffee I make at home to the drive-throughs, walk-ins, and quick kiosks inside grocery stores and hotels. While in Seattle, I had to make time in my schedule to see the first Starbucks. I am not alone.

A line at Starbucks isn't that out of the ordinary. As a consistent drinker of "coffee black," I often grumble in line behind other, time-consuming, complex orders that sound more like an ice cream sundae than a cup of coffee. The line at the first Starbucks is out of control. It snakes out the door and down the block. Once inside, as you gaze at framed newspaper articles and vintage coffee bean sacks—trappings you might find in any original small business location—the line forks. There's a line that sorts into three registers where you order drinks and souvenirs from this sacred place. And another line for those waiting for their coffee. There's an employee directing traffic.

As I stood there taking it in, I was looking for something. Something different and amazing. Outside of the line, nothing was that remarkable about the store. It was a Starbucks. All the people making this store a part of their day, a part of their vacation or work trip, a part of their life was what was different. Maybe they were all looking, too.

That's because Starbucks means something to us.

Logos, Logotherapy, and Brownies

After one of my talks about branding, I'm often met offstage by people with their chests puffed out and a big smile on their face. They lean forward with pride and say, "We just rebranded." As they rock back, they add: "Ye-e-e-e-ep. We just redid our whole logo." With an awkward grin frozen on my face, I nod along and look for a way to change the subject. "Where did you get that brownie?"

That's because it takes all of my powers not to conjure Mandy Patinkin's Inigo Montoya from *The Princess Bride*, whose *second* most iconic line states in response to another character's continued use of the word *inconceivable,* "You keep using that word. I do not think it means what you think it means."[2]

Branding is your logo, right? If your brand's broken, you must need a better logo. If you're looking to reinvigorate your brand, try a jazzy new logo. Why does everyone make this branding stuff so hard?

This thinking is, of course, shortsighted. Your brand is so much more than your logo. And that's what we're going to look at as we unpack the seven Brand Now Dynamics. At the risk of confusing you, logo is a good place to start. Or more specifically, its root, in the Ancient Greek logos.

Actually, logos meant a lot of things in Greek including "ground," "plea," "opinion," "expectation," "word," and "discourse."[3] It became a more technical term as the philosopher Heraclitus used the term for a principle of order and knowledge. Logos is the logic behind an argument. Persuade an audience using logical arguments and supportive evidence. Logos helps us unlock meaning.

And meaning matters. A thinker who means a lot to me is Viktor Frankl, an Austrian neurologist, psychiatrist, and Holocaust survivor. His own hellish experiences led him to discover the importance of finding meaning in all forms of existence, even the most brutal ones. Frankl went on to found logotherapy. I initially assumed logotherapy was a cool psychological grounding for branding and logos. I was slightly let down to discover that it's actually a form of existential analysis. As it turns out, it can help us, too.

One of logotherapy's key principles asserts that our main motivation for living is our will to find meaning in life. According to Frankl, one of the ways in which we discover meaning is by experiencing something or encountering someone.[4] Which brings us back to brands.

We are overwhelmed by stimuli in today's distracted digital world, which is why we want to create brands that stand out. But we miss something in the earliest stages of brand development. We stunt our work by failing to provide meaning. Nigel Hollis is Chief Global Analyst at Kantar Millward Brown, a market research firm focused on advertising effectiveness, strategic communication, media, and brand-equity research. He's also the author of *The Meaningful Brand*. In his research, Hollis has noted that less than 25 percent of brands are seen by shoppers as distinctive.[5]

Too often this leads us to the Marketing 101 staple: differentiation. How is your brand different from mine? This sets the bar too low. Instead of just differentiating your brand from what else is out there, you need to create meaning. When I interviewed New Zealand–based brand strategist Mark Di Somma, he noted, "You have to build an understanding both inside your walls and outside of your walls. You have to build something people want to interact with."[6] You have to build something with meaning. A brand that stands for something. Whether you're a multinational conglomerate selling consumer packaged goods or a realtor selling houses, your brand has to mean something to those you serve. Why should someone care more about your products? Why should I buy a house from you? A brand with meaning answers these questions seamlessly.

If you follow this back to my awkward conversation with someone who's rebranded with a new logo—pre-brownie pivot—I'll cede that, of course, your logo is a part of your brand; but ultimately that's just one expression. From the Greek logos to Frankl, Hollis, and Di Somma, to build a standout brand, you must be grounded in meaning. Beyond the services you provide and the products you sell. Meaning has many definitions, but most useful are those that cite endowing something with "purpose or significance."[7]

So, where can your brand find purpose and significance?

Start with Your People

Meaning comes from your audience because meaning is ultimately created by your audience. That's what makes all this so hard. As brands, we can set things in motion, but the real meaning, the connections, come from your audience—your people, your stakeholders.

Yet it's easy to sit in your darkened brand cave crafting the perfect message. Standout brands know that their strength comes from their audience. To create meaning, you have to first understand your people. As Lululemon notes on their website, they make "technical athletic clothes for yoga, running, working out, and most other sweaty pursuits." Based on this alone, you get a general idea on who their customers are. But Lululemon looked deeper.

CUSTOMER A   CUSTOMER B

They looked past traditional demographic personas and created stories for their ideal female and male customers—Ocean and Duke, respectively. Ocean is a 32-year-old professional single woman who makes $100,000 a year. She is "engaged, has her own condo, is traveling, fashionable, has an hour and a half to work out a day," says founder Chip Wilson. Duke is 35, makes a bit more money, enjoys surfing in the summer and snowboarding in the winter, and is willing to pay more for quality.[8] These aspirational customer archetypes speak to the meaning these customers are searching for in their lives. Meaning that Lululemon can take on in the real-life Oceans and Dukes in the world.

As I relayed the stories of Ocean and Duke to my MBA students at the University of Iowa, a few rolled their eyes. However, in discussion the following week, one student raised her hand, saying that she'd talked with a very Ocean-like friend of hers who said that even when she couldn't afford Lululemon, the brand represented where she wanted to be in her life. She wanted to be Ocean. Demographics and personas are great for segmenting your marketing, but to create meaning you have to tease this out even further. Try adding qualitative insights and psychographics to your quantitative demography like age, gender, and income.

A brand is more than something you buy: it's an ethos you buy into. BarkBox is a box-based subscription service for dog owners, sending them pet-themed products and technology each month. Early in the life of this innovative brand, cofounder Henrik Werdelin realized there's a difference between a dog owner and a dog parent: "Dog parents are people who really love their dogs. Unfortunately, there aren't many places they can go to find new ways to delight their dog. BarkBox is full of those things."[9] This subtle shift in nomenclature—dog parents instead of dog owners—does a lot. It tells you about their customers and how BarkBox aims to serve them.

A brand has to be something that you want to join. Meaning fosters connection and creates belonging, which is important. In another classroom discussion on brand communities, cars came up. One student noted that she was a longtime MINI owner who winsomely shared that she had just switched to Jeep. I smiled, telling her that her choices are two of the best examples of customer communities in the automotive sector. Both brands have secret languages for customers to communicate with other drivers and regular owner-club meetups. Both brands have cultivated strong emotions in the hearts and minds of their customers.

Some take this customer focus and alignment even further. Amazon founder and CEO Jeff Bezos famously leaves an empty chair at the conference-room table, informing meeting attendees that they need to consider that seat occupied by their customer, "the most important person in the room."[10] You have to understand your customer first in order to create meaning. Not just their age and income, but what they care about. What matters to them and what they want out of life. Can you make your brand's meaning a part of their quest for meaning?

Grounding your brand with meaning can sound daunting. But at the end of the day you have to connect with your customers in one of two ways.

Creating Meaning in the Head and the Heart

The 1992 U.S. presidential election was disrupted by a standout political brand in the form of a third-party candidate, Texas billionaire H. Ross Perot. Splitting the conservative vote, Perot ultimately created an opening for an insurgent governor from Arkansas. For his running mate, Perot chose Vice Admiral James Stockdale, who had a certain way with words.

As always, *Saturday Night Live* was responsible for some of the best political satire of the time. In a sketch featuring Dana Carvey as Perot and the late, great Phil Hartman as Stockdale, Perot ran on with his political ideas while a zoned-out Stockdale blurted—as he did in an actual debate—"Who am I? Why am I here?!?" While these non-sequitur questions did no favors for the Perot-Stockdale ticket, they can be useful to you as a brand-builder. "Who am I? Why am I here?!?" seems like an obvious question. Especially in business. "I'm ABC Widget Company and I'm here to sell widgets to the people that build things with widgets. What else is there?"

Sure, a simple answer like this might be how you fill out your business organization papers and legal filings, but it doesn't help you answer the bigger question—why am I here? As many of us struggle with this question in life, it's no wonder it's a challenge professionally as we work to build standout brands.

As John Michael Morgan, brand strategist and author of *Brand Against the Machine*, says: "We often think that what we sell is the product. We're actually selling the in-between."[11] The in-between is everything, including customer service, culture, leadership, and more. What we're ultimately doing as a brand is often much bigger than the widget that we make or the industry we're in. What we're really doing is something bigger. That's where we find meaning. In her book *What Great Brands Do*, Denise Lee Yohn suggests that great brands need to focus on answering that bigger question, not just "What business are you in?" but delving deeper and looking at what business you're *really* in.[12]

In the scrappy brand blueprint I sketched out in *Get Scrappy*, I suggested that strong brands start with a spark. A reason for being. Like Yohn and Morgan, I caution you not to merely check the box for the SIC code your business is filed under. I called this the brand spark. Based on what your customers' needs are and what desires they have, why are you *really* here?

For example, if you were to define Disney as a business, you would peg them as an entertainment empire (movies, theme parks, cruises, etc.). But that's not how Disney defines their brand: They're in the magic business. They create magical experiences. Apple was always bigger than computer hardware and software: it was about the intersection of arts and technology. Zappos is literally a derivative of the Spanish word for shoes (zapatos), but they've never been just a shoe company: they've always offered legendary service. Based on these brand sparks, you can see that these brands are about something bigger. They're about what matters to the customer. What's meaningful.

There are many different ways to create meaning for your customers. Thinking of all the different emotional desires and responses people can have becomes overwhelming fast. To make this manageable, remember that most of branding and marketing is about appealing to the hearts and minds of customers. Let's take a look at how you can create meaning in the head and the heart.

HEAD: An appeal to the head is an appeal that makes sense. Something that's the smarter play. A brand that's doing something in a new and/or inventive way. Or perhaps a brand that's defined by smart content. Within appeals to the head, you can find the familiar advantages of saving time and money as well as convenience. Dollar Shave Club's subscription razor service offers smart savings of both time and money when compared to traditional store-bought cartridges.

Other head appeals include:

- → **Curation.** StitchFix selects clothing items so you don't have to shop.
- → **Flexibility.** Zappos takes back shoes—even after you've worn them.
- → **Safety.** Tylenol famously recalled their pain reliever in the 1980s because they knew safety had been compromised.
- → **Simplicity.** Field Notes focuses on being the best little notepad and offers few, if any, brand extensions.
- → **Timeliness.** Amazon Dash buttons send you Tide so you don't have to go to the store.

HEART: When we talk about emotional appeals, most of us think first of the heart. This is something that we have strong feelings about—either for or against. A brand that appeals to our heart makes us feel a certain way. You're happy, excited, attractive. You feel better after encountering the brand than you did before. When you enter a Jaguar dealership, you feel different. You feel luxurious because of the way you're treated when you walk through the door.

Other heart appeals include:

- → **Belonging.** Remember my student who was a MINI owner, then a Jeep owner? She felt a sense of belonging in both communities.

→ **Humor.** When you laugh looking at the napkins at Jimmy John's, which announce in bold lettering—WIPE!

→ **Nostalgia.** It makes you feel retro to kick around in a pair of Chuck Taylor Converse All-Stars.

→ **Responsible.** You feel better buying a pair of shoes from a company like Tom's because you know they sent another pair to someone in need.

→ **Style.** You feel a bit cooler wearing your Ray-Ban Aviators than the pair you got at a gas station.

Meaning can also be hidden. Most think IKEA is a powerful brand because they offer home furnishings that are relatively cheap and somewhat easy to assemble. But there's more to it than that. In 2011, researchers Michael I. Norton of Harvard Business School, Daniel Mochon of Yale, and Dan Ariely of Duke shared their finding that we actually like brands like IKEA because we had to do a bit of work. "The IKEA Effect" is a cognitive bias in which consumers place a disproportionately high value on products that they've partially created. As Norton, Mochon, and Ariely note, "Labor alone can be sufficient to induce greater liking for the fruits of one's labor: even constructing a standardized bureau, an arduous, solitary task, can lead people to overvalue their (often poorly constructed) creations."[13]

If you're stuck within the constraints of your industry or sector, consider a simple "extraction" exercise from Jay Acunzo, former Google employee and host of the *Unthinkable* podcast. "Find something from outside of your echo chamber or industry that you admire and you extract the aspects of their brand that make them exceptional. For example, you may want to be the Anthony Bourdain of business. How would you go about doing this?"[14]

It's not enough to just answer the question of what your business does. If you want to build a standout brand, you have to have meaning in the hearts and minds of your customers. It's not that you're answering two disparate questions. Brand strategy and your overall business strategy are very much related.

As Erich Joachimsthaler, founder and CEO of global strategy firm Vivaldi and coauthor of *Brand Leadership,* notes, "On the front end, you have the brand. On the back end, you have the overall business strategy." You have to have both clearly defined to succeed and stand out today. As Joachimsthaler goes on to say, "In the future, we'll have an inner sanctum—an inner circle—of brands who we'll rely on more and more."[15]

Should Your Brand Take a Stand?

Exploring the head and the heart even further, we get into territory that's often scary for businesses today. Should your brand stand for something? This, too, is easy to mistake as a simple question. Of course, we want our brands to stand for something. However, as we venture beyond the safe confines of product and industry conversations, broader sociological, cultural, and political implications can present a challenge.

Sometimes it's easier not to take a stand. Strong beliefs give our brands sharp edges that we naturally feel we need to round off. Those with a balance sheet–first mind-set often point out here that taking a stance in these politically and socially charged times gives 50 percent of the population a reason *not* to buy what you're selling. That's why it's become accepted that politics and social issues are a "third rail" in business, something to avoid at all costs.

On the other hand, modern consumers are overwhelmed with thousands of brand impressions each day. We have a clutter problem. Consumers today aren't just looking for brands to purchase from. Especially the coveted millennial demographic. They're looking for communities to be a part of. Brands worth belonging to are the ones that appeal to us emotionally. It's a delicate balance. Just what should your brand stand for, and when?

"Brands that we look to, that are charismatic, know their audience. They know who they are," says Carla Johnson, coauthor of *Experiences: The 7th Era of Marketing*.[16] If you've fleshed out who your audience is, start extrapolating even further. What matters most to them socially or even politically?

In September 2014, CVS Pharmacy turned heads by announcing that the chain would no longer be selling cigarettes. "By eliminating the sale of cigarettes and tobacco products in our stores, we can make a difference in the health of all Americans," CVS CEO Larry Merlo said when the ban took effect. Health is at the very heart of the CVS brand.[17]

Thinx makes period-proof underwear. In addition to adopting an authentic, transparent brand voice on what some consider a taboo topic, Thinx regularly shares updates on women's health issues and feminism in their email newsletter. One edition featured a Texas judge ruling that doctors could refuse care on grounds of religious freedom, along with a summary of artists not performing at the Trump inauguration. Feminism and women's health are cornerstones of the Thinx brand.

Tea Collection is a children's clothing company with globally inspired designs. Following the 2016 presidential election, they sent an impassioned email to their customers expressing concerns on President Trump's xenophobic rhetoric. "We want to open up the world for all children—to celebrate the common humanity that we share with all people, no matter the color of our skin or the nationality of our birth." A diverse, global perspective is at the core of the Tea brand.

Luvvie Ajayi is an author, speaker, and digital strategist. As she notes, she "thrives at the intersection of comedy, technology, and activism."[18] A simple Venn diagram on her website's About page reinforces this. This could be a useful exercise for your brand. Draw overlapping circles and use them to answer—who you are, who you serve, and what you stand for.

Ultimately, a brand that stands for something stands out. Isn't that what we're all looking to do?

Being an Authentic, Meaningful Brand

There are many different ways to create meaning. Ultimately, in the immortal words of that nautical great Popeye, "I yam what I yam." Regardless of how you endow your brand with meaning, you have to be true to who you are as an organization. Many brands have fallen short by trying to be someone or something that they ultimately weren't.

In the wake of a contentious political environment, many brands advertising in Super Bowl LI in 2017 adopted a more socially progressive message. From Airbnb to Audi, many brands chose to wear their hearts on their sleeves, featuring messages of inclusion and patriotism. However not all were met with the same response.

The early buzz went to Anheuser-Busch for their ad telling the immigrant story of founder Adolphus Busch coming to America. Many cried out, as they felt betrayed by the beer brand for the everyman. (Maybe they forgot to sketch out the Venn diagram described earlier.) This was in contrast to Coke, who ran an ad called "It's Beautiful," featuring "America the Beautiful" sung by a variety of people in a variety of languages. As I watched the ad, it felt familiar. That's because it wasn't a new ad. They'd run it in the Super Bowl three years earlier. It was not only more relevant in 2017, but it also aligned with who Coke is—and has always been—as a brand.

Coke has long promoted a global perspective dating back to 1971's "Hilltop" ad ("I'd like to teach the world to sing . . ."). For all the attention that the Anheuser-Busch immigrant ad got, it wasn't as tied to who they are and, more importantly, what their customers want. "It's Beautiful" wasn't a pivot for Coke but rather a reinforcement of their very consistent brand. It also generated some of the most ad-related tweets during the game. Granted, not all were positive, as some called to #BoycottCoke.[19] However, as discussed earlier, standing up as a brand is important and ultimately leads to stronger, positive ties.

Sometimes the best strategy isn't a radical departure. Sometimes it's surprisingly simple. To class things up a bit in case you think less of me for quoting Popeye, as Oscar Wilde said, "Be yourself. Everyone else is already taken." Find meaning that you—and you alone—can lay claim to. Authenticity matters more than ever in the digital age. More on that in the chapters ahead.

The cornerstone for building a standout brand lies in meaning. As Park Howell, founder of the Business of Story platform, says, "What do you do as a brand? Your whole job is to create meaning around your brand and connect that to people's lives. To make their lives better. To empower them. Not just sell them some crap."[20] Look for a way that you can consistently create meaning in the hearts and minds of your customers, and you'll be rewarded for years to come.

Now let's pause for our first set of building blocks before we move on to the next chapter, where we'll look at how we build what we're building.

BUILDING BLOCKS

- Create a persona for your ideal customer. Go beyond demographics. What do they care about? What matters most to them?

- Have some fun. Can you create a unique name for your customers like BarkBox did with their "dog parents"?

- Take a page from Amazon. Try leaving an empty chair or another symbolic reminder for your customers in your next meeting. Did anything interesting come from it?

- Based on what you learn about your customers, what is your brand's spark? What is your reason for doing what you do? Remember, it's not necessarily the business you're in: it's something bigger. If you need help, remember the different ways to appeal to their head and heart.

- Is there a social or political movement that matters to your audience? Does your brand belong there, taking a stand alongside them?

- Try an extraction by filling in the blanks. We are the _____ (insert aspirational brand from outside your echo chamber) of _____ (insert your industry).

TWO
Structure

In his book *To Sell Is Human*, best-selling author Daniel H. Pink cites research dating back to the 1920s that states that when it comes to dealing with others, there's more than just being an extrovert or an introvert. It's a spectrum on which most fall in the middle. He calls them *ambiverts*. "They're not overly extroverted. They're not overly introverted. They're a little of both."[1]

Similarly, most are familiar with the right and left hemispheres of the brain and what they mean. When I say "I'm very left-brained," you're able to infer that I'm data-driven and analytical—linear and organized in my thinking. When I say "I'm super right-brained," you know that I'm creative and intuitive—imaginative and in touch with my feelings. So in the world of work, we tend to assume that the business folks are left-brained and the creative folks are right-brained.

Wrong. In fact, a recent study from the University of Utah goes even further, noting that we aren't preferential with one hemisphere of the brain. Most of us exist somewhere in between.[2] And many of those in-betweeners are working in branding and marketing. If you're reading this book, that last statement is either affirming or frightening to you.

Those in the latter frightened group picked up this book because branding is something you need help with, as you often find yourself saying, "I am not a creative person." Science just shot this down. Your brain is just as creative as mine! Those in the former group, who felt a sense of affirmation, are probably like me, meaning you describe yourself as an organized creative person. An example of just how squarely I sit at the hemispheric borderline? I majored in psychology and theatre arts.

Why the foray into the human brain? Well, first I was a psych major, so it's fun. It's also a logical segue from the advanced inner workings of meaning. Now that you've staked out real estate to own in the hearts and minds of your customers, what's next? Building the brand.

Building the brand. Brand-building. Like peanut butter and jelly, the verb *building* is paired with the word *brand* almost unconsciously. But we can't make assumptions here either. Brand-building is both an art and science.

Re-Sequencing Your Brand DNA

As a self-proclaimed "word nerd," I have no problems whatsoever wading into the tall grass of semantics. Especially on a topic as squishy and ill-defined as branding. In fact, let's start there—with the word *branding*.

Categorically, I'm fine with branding as a bucket to talk about what we do in a general sense. But if we want to get more specific,

I'm less comfortable with this label for the simple reason that it conjures up all of that dated definition of branding things physically. From marking our products with a branding iron to marketing at consumers with traditional advertising, all this feels ill-fitting for the task at hand.

We're not just branding things. We're building brands in the hearts and minds of our customers. And you can't do that with a hot iron or broadcast media alone. Today's consumer is dynamic and digital. What we're building is no longer linear or logical. In the past, continuing the brand-building metaphor literally has been helpful. That's why we dig foundations, add levels, and trim and finish our structures. We know how to do that. We've been building sand castles and snow forts since we were kids.

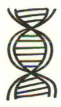

To paraphrase *Breaking Bad's* Walter White, as brand-builders you have to respect the science. It may not be a linear or logical structure that you're building. Instead, think of all the pieces of DNA that go into creating your brand, all the molecules or touchpoints that make your brand what it is today.

Touchpoints like your . . .

→ Logo
→ Slogan
→ Business cards
→ Products and packaging
→ Advertising—both broadcast and digital
→ Direct mail

→ Email marketing
→ Signage
→ And more

It's more than all of this, but it's made up of everything. (Note: A comprehensive Touchpoint Checklist can be found in the Brand Now Toolbox.) Like the individual pieces of DNA that contain genetic information, each of these pieces says something about your brand but isn't the full story—to say nothing of the fact that you no longer know in what order your consumers are encountering your various touchpoints.

In a world where you have infinite platforms on which to interact with your consumers, it's increasingly challenging to structure who you are and what you stand for. One way to start is by making a list of all these into pieces of your brand DNA.

Now let's blow up the list.

Checklists, Dimmer Switches, and Divining Rods

As an educator/consultant/author/speaker/parent of five/husband of one, I have a lot to do. Lists help me get all my work done. Lists can also be critical in your work as a brand-builder. Honestly, I don't really want you to blow your list up. But I do want you to blow up *how* you've built branding lists in the past. In *Get Scrappy*, I cautioned against checklist marketing—the dangerous practice of checking digital channels off as though they were items on an arbitrary list. There's no one-size-fits-all approach to branding and marketing. Your brand structure is as unique as your DNA. Forgot what anyone else is doing. Especially in your industry.

Grounded with the meaning you want to create, consider all the ways you could bring this to life. To do this, it might help to take a scientific break from our DNA sequencing. Think of your brand's structure as a light switch with dimmers (also known as rheostats) for every possible brand touchpoint. You can turn some all the way up and others all the way down—while others still can be left partially up or down. You have innumerable options.

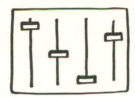

Before you get the nervous sweats thinking about the infinite combinations (*What's he doing?!? He's not making this any easier!*), let's apply some very simple logic to what you turn up and down on your brand's dimmer switch. If you think about your brand's meaning, you can expand upon this to develop your brand promise. More than a trite slogan or tagline, your brand promise answers this question: What do you do, and for whom? This brand promise can guide you in determining which dimmer switches to turn up and down.

In the last chapter, we looked at Zappos's commitment to service. The brand promise, "Powered by Service," sits below their logo in almost every instance. This intrinsic meaning informs the structure and weighted importance of their brand touchpoints. For example, the dimmer switches of their TV ads are turned down. Almost completely off. But their customer service emails are second to none. When the sole suddenly peeled off of a new pair of boots I had recently purchased, I cried foul and received an immediate and personal response.

As the email signature reinforces, they're powered by service. That's why they responded immediately and with empathy. They understood that I'd already been inconvenienced so they didn't bother with a labor-intensive return procedure. They even had

TO: NICK WESTERGAARD
FROM: ZAPPOS.COM
SUBJECT: YOUR BOOTS

Dear Nick Westergaard,

Thank you for shopping at Zappos.com. We are very sorry for any frustration that has been caused with your order. As we feel you have been troubled enough already, we do not want to inconvenience you further with the hassle of having to return the below merchandise.

Kenneth Cole Reaction: Close 4 Comfort in Black, 11

Please feel free to keep that merchandise, donate it to charity, turn it into an art project, or whatever else you may want to do. Your original payment method has been refunded in full for that and you will see that credit of $_____ within 2–10 business days, as soon as your bank authorizes that credit. Your account has also been noted accordingly to show that you have been advised not to return the above item to us. You may also save this e-mail for your own records, if you wish.

Sincerely,
Ryan
The Zappos Customer Loyalty Team
Zappos.com
Powered by Service
1-800-ZAPPOS-1 (1-800-927-7671) or 702-943-7677
e-mail: cs@zappos.com
http://www.zappos.com

some fun with this by noting that I could "keep that merchandise, donate it to charity, turn it into an art project, or whatever else you may want to do." Even the humor is delicately handled. While some fun customer service communications may have opted for more, Zappos carefully balanced humor with empathy.

Trunk Club is a personalized mid- to high-end men's and women's clothing service based in Chicago. Each customer or member works with a stylist who curates a box of clothes, which the customer can either keep or return. My wife recently signed up; and when she received her first delivery, she cried out from the next room. Thinking that we were in imminent danger, I rushed in. "What? What??" She turned to me and, with a smile on her face normally reserved for cute kittens, said, "Isn't it adorable how the box looks like a trunk?"

Once my heart rate returned to normal, I acknowledged that, yes, it was adorable. But it was also an extremely significant touchpoint for a high-end clothing brand whose store you'll never set foot in. Boxes may not be as critical for brands with an in-person retail experience like Banana Republic, but for virtual brands such as Trunk Club and eyeglasses disruptor Warby Parker, they are paramount. That's why many online brands turn their in-person touchable touchpoints way up on their dimmer switches.

Curated clothing-box clubs are one of my wife's favorite personal treats. In the grand scheme of things, this is a pretty healthful treat compared to, say, donuts—which are my personal treat of choice. A friend commented once on the prevalence of donuts in my Instagram feed, noting that "Donuts are your kryptonite." It's true. Having a great day? Let's celebrate with a donut. Having a bad day? Better fix it with a donut.

One of the more unique donut haunts in my neck of the woods is Hurts Donut Company. With locations throughout the Midwest and more on the way, Hurts Donut specializes in "whimsical donuts," including donuts made with Nutella and their infamous "Cereal Killers" topped with everything from Fruit Loops to Cinnamon Toast Crunch. My personal favorite is one simply called "The Jesus," which is swirled with cinnamon and vanilla frosting because, as the description card below the donut says, "Jesus died for our cinnamon. . . ."

[Editor's Note: At this point, the author left his laptop and went to the aforementioned donut shop. When he returned, after pacing around his office on a sugar high, he continued with the following.]

With an engaging menu, a logo featuring a donut with a bandage (Hurts Donut—get it?), and a food truck in the form of a converted ambulance, Hurts Donut creates an amazing experience from a few key touchpoints. For example, its coffee mug is garnished with a set of brass knuckles as the handle (Hurts Donut—get it?). Should a coffee cup be on your brand's dimmer switch? Probably not. However, if you're in the business of whimsical donuts, you'd better pair it with a whimsical cup of coffee.

Use the meaning you create with your spark and brand promise as a divining rod or compass, leading you to which touchpoints are most important, most critical for who you are and what you stand for.

Structure is variable. And sometimes you can create a stand-out brand structurally by avoiding some traditional touchpoints altogether.

Dimmers Down: The Rise of the Alternative Brand

With a donut habit like mine, I've got to do something to keep the pounds off. Luckily, I love running. Plus, I can catch up on my favorite podcasts while doing it. When my old over-the-ear aviation-style headphones bit it, I thought it might be time to join the twenty-first century and invest in a more modern yet durable Bluetooth set.

Like many of us would, I turned to my friends on Facebook: Which headphones are best for running? Friends suggested big players like Beats by Dre and other well-known brands. Ultimately, I decided to go with a lesser known but well-rated brand: Status Audio.

A friend recommended Status Audio headphones as a low-cost, high-quality solution for electronics gear that most runners are hard on. The sound quality is crisp, the Bluetooth connectivity is great. I even loved the Spartan packaging, which coyly noted "no logos, no celebrities—just sound." Structurally they are a very different brand, opting to turn down some of the more common dimmer switches employed by their big-name competition (celebrity hype, etc.).

As you'll learn in the chapter on Clarity, making something better isn't always additive. Sometimes you're subtracting—taking away traditional branding elements and standing out as a result. In its golden years, the automotive industry was exemplary of traditional brand advertising. Big, bold brands producing big, bold ads that they reinforced to the masses with big, bold budgets. Tesla Motors has taken a different approach. The electric-vehicle company famously has a $0 marketing budget. They have no advertising, no ad agency, no CMO, and no dealer network.[3] And it's working out pretty well for them.

It's not that Tesla isn't doing any brand-building. They've just turned most of the traditional automotive dimmer switches (ads and dealers) way down as they've turned others way up. Because of their decision to avoid costly dealer networks, Tesla is able to control the dealership experience. The high-tech stores offer customers a hassle-free experience where they can learn and ask questions instead of the stereotypical hard-driving sales environment many expect from a car dealership. "Right now, the stores are our advertising," spokeswoman Alexis Georgeson told *Advertising Age*.[4]

And what better voice for the brand than its cofounder, tech billionaire Elon Musk? He's as cool as Tony Stark (he was reportedly an inspiration for Robert Downey Jr's portrayal of Marvel's infamous genius billionaire playboy philanthropist). And he has more than 10 million Twitter followers.[5] What better public personification of the brand than the person behind the brand with his own, very big megaphone?

Sometimes brand structure is dictated by marketing models. Best practices for digital marketing say that a brand should create content on its website and then share that content on other social networks. Online media giant BuzzFeed has websites spanning a variety of news and entertainment topics including politics, animals, business, and food. With their own dedicated BuzzFeed Food site, it seemed odd to some when they launched a new brand of videos uploaded directly to social networks such as Facebook and YouTube, skipping the step of driving traffic to the media property itself.

With Tasty, BuzzFeed focused on quick (most videos are a minute or less), high-quality videos showing people how to make comfort food. At the end of each video, a male voice is heard laughing as he says "Oh, yes!" The fun paid off as each Tasty video regularly gets tens of millions of views. This success has led to spin-offs such

as the internationally inspired Proper Tasty, one of the fastest-growing Facebook pages that BuzzFeed has launched, gathering 3.7 million followers and more than 190 million video views in just a month.[6]

These brands are everywhere, like Sriracha sauce from Huy Fong Foods. Even if you haven't had it, I bet you'd recognize its distinct rooster-clad red bottle. (Even Jude recognizes this!) Same with the infinitely useful household spray, WD-40. Both have rich meaning and yet both eschew the traditional structural components of branding. Neither runs ads. Neither is targeting you with huge marketing campaigns. No clever slogans. All the regular branding dimmer switches are down, but they've turned their packaging way up.

Powerful brands such as Status, Tesla, Tasty, Sriracha, and WD-40 are hiding in plain sight everywhere. Some might call them "anti-brands." I don't like this label, because they're still branding: they're just doing so very differently. They're not anti-brands: they're alternative brands. And they can be very formidable in today's crowded digital marketplace. In fact, as Robert V. Kozinets of the Kellogg School of Management at Northwestern University posits, many consumers today are increasingly distressed enough by today's noisy markets that they're looking to emancipate themselves from it.[7]

The only danger of being an alternative brand? If you turn your major dimmer switches way down or off entirely, make sure you compensate by turning other switches up. I'll be honest, the first time I recommended my new Status headphones to someone else, I struggled to recall the name. If you're subtracting brand DNA, make sure you're adding it elsewhere.

If you want your consumers to remember who you are and what you stand for, you have to help them. That's where patterns can come in handy.

Creating Brand Patterns

As brand-builders, we're in the business of understanding and hopefully altering human behavior. That's no small task. Especially in an overstimulated environment. Luckily, we have a timeless tool at our disposal to help.

Few cognitive abilities have had the impact on the human species that pattern recognition has. At a very basic level, it helps us match new stimuli to insights we've already observed. It helped the early hunters and gatherers know where to hunt and where to gather, based on where they'd seen animals and plants previously. Patterns help us make our way through the world and solve the problems we encounter along the way. Researchers from the University of Texas at Austin found that when we're uncertain, we often create patterns where none exist as a means of making sense of the world.[8]

If the world is noisy and patterns are useful tools for making sense of it all, shouldn't you be using patterns to help your brand stand out? Absolutely. Branding has been disrupted in many ways. Instead of being linear, our communications are chaotic—starting and stopping without a clearly defined beginning, middle, and end. Where broadcast media was unidirectional, defined as one loud voice speaking to many, our new media environment is multi-directional. In many cases, our brand voice comes from many different sources at many different times. We're less and less in control of how consumers learn about our brands. To bring order from this chaos, we need to use patterns.

"To succeed in a more agile world, a brand needs to think less about defining a fixed identity and more about creating coherent and flexible patterns," says Marc Shillum, founder of Chief Creative Office and author of the *Brands as Patterns* manifesto.[9]

Consider Google's most recent identity shift. While much attention was given to the new streamlined typography and retirement of their severely serifed and difficult-to-scale logotype, they also simplified the brand identity into a series of patterns. A simple logo and logotype supported by four very basic colors. These four colors are found throughout the Android mobile experience, in the icon of their multi-platform Chrome browser, and more. This is a subtle yet powerful pattern that reinforces the Google brand throughout its many diverse applications.

Patterns are both consistent and flexible. Consistent repetition, even with variation, helps a brand with patterns remain top-of-mind. This aids recall; but there's more to it than that. "Repetition can build top-of-mind recognition, but variation creates relevance," says Shillum.[10]

Trace this back to Google, and you can see that their brand's elasticity is made possible through patterns. The familiarity we get from patterns also builds trust, which is increasingly important in our connected yet disconnected digital world. It was the use of patterns that got Pavlov's dogs salivating on command. In this signature study of classical conditioning, when the scientists rung the bell while presenting food, the dogs would salivate. Over time, they were able to get the dogs to salivate with the bell alone, sans food.

Before you laugh at a comparison to Pavlov's dogs, remember that, like me, you probably eagerly scan your front porch as you return home. My wife and I have both noted that as we pull into the driveway, our eyes are drawn to the front door to see if "Santa" (our nickname for Amazon) has been there. Amazon has us all conditioned with their patterns of consistently creating an offline outcome as the result of a virtual interaction. And it was pattern recognition that helped my toddler son recognize the Starbucks brand as "coffee" at a young age.

So how can you use brand patterns? Like Google, you can consider the visual basics of color and design. You can also create expectations around the content that you create. A new blog post is published every Monday and a podcast on Wednesday. Or maybe you produce a podcast season, as many are doing in the wake of breakout hits *Serial* and *S-Town*. Or, taking a page from Amazon, you can condition with consistent online and offline interaction and behavior.

In many cases, you may already have patterns at work throughout your brand. Things you say. Things you do. Certain ways of expressing yourself. This is a good start. To build on this even further, identify and isolate these patterns. Communicate them to others on your team so that they can continue to use them in their work. The only way you can increase your audience's recognition of the patterns you create is by making them even stronger and using them more consistently. This takes work. Patterns start small but can deliver big results as you implement them throughout your brand experience. We'll come back to touchpoints and patterns when we approach our seventh and final dynamic, Experience.

Structure is an important step in brand-building, but structure is changing. All these pieces of your brand DNA—your dimmer switches, touchpoints, and patterns—come together to help you tell your story.

You have meaning. You have structure. Now what are you going to say?

BUILDING BLOCKS

- Your brand DNA isn't like anyone else's. Start with your spark (why are you here?) and brand promise (what you do for whom), and use that to guide the sequencing of your brand's DNA.

- Remember, it's a dimmer switch (fade some things up and others down), as opposed to falling prey to a generic checklist approach.

- List your brand's touchpoints. Now, using a scale of 1 to 5, rate them in order of relevance to your brand promise—1 is most relevant, 5 is least relevant. Look at your top three most relevant touchpoints. What can you do to amplify these touchpoints even further? For help, see the Touchpoint Checklist in the Brand Now Toolbox.

- Try flipping this the other way. Are there traditional brand touchpoints others in your industry use that you could turn down or off entirely on your dimmer switch? Can you stand out by zigging where others are zagging?

- Take a look at the brand touchpoints that you've mapped. Are there recognizable patterns? How can you reinforce them to make them even more recognizable?

THREE
Story

As the father of five kids, I've told my share of stories at bedtime. Often, I'm reading from our colossal library of children's books. I'm fairly certain I have *The Lorax* committed to memory. Sometimes I even make up my own ("The Story of Today" is a nonfiction favorite, recounting the events of the day from the point of view of the child I'm telling the story to). Stories are a great ritual for closing the day together.

Stories are also powerful patterns learned at a young age. From your parents reading you books to sharing tall tales and jokes around campfires and watercoolers, you know how stories work. They have a beginning, middle, and end. Stories are patterns that represent the intersection of meaning and structure. You know who you are and what you stand for. You know which structural elements matter most for your brand.

Now what? Now it's story time once again.

At the end of the day, we're all in the storytelling business. Whether you're a marketing professional at a Fortune 500 company, running a small business, fund-raising for a nonprofit, or communicating on behalf of a government agency, you're responsible for telling your brand's story with the intention of producing a result.

It's worth noting that those stories told earlier in life had results-driven intentions, too. However, in a professional context, "getting the kids to sleep" and "making Adam laugh so hard the milk comes out his nose" have been replaced with "creating brand awareness" and "driving leads and sales."

In recent years, storytelling has become something of a buzzword in business circles. *We need to tell better stories. . . . It's all about framing our story. . . .* These statements are nebulous unless there's a shared understanding for why storytelling works and how we can tell better stories, both online and off.

The Science of Storytelling

"Story is about trying to make sense out of the confusion, chaos, and terror of being a human being," says Robert McKee, writing instructor and author of *Story: Substance, Structure, Style and the Principles of Screenwriting.*[1] McKee's popular "Story Seminar" has inspired Hollywood screenwriters like Peter Jackson, Paul Haggis, and the entire writing staff at Pixar. John Cleese has attended McKee's seminar three times.[2]

As it turns out, our brains are hardwired for comprehending stories. A few important things happen in the brain in response to a story. First, two key areas of the brain are activated—Broca's and Wernicke's areas (speech production and understanding of written and spoken language, respectively). A well-told story can engage many additional areas, including the motor and frontal cortex.

Stories activate parts of the brain that allow listeners to turn stories into their own ideas using a process called neural coupling.[3] You want your customers to be a part of your brand and your ideas? Tell stories. Listening to stories even creates similar brain activity

between the listener and the speaker. Want to get everyone on the same page? Tell stories. "When someone tells a story, we're connected," says Nancy Duarte, CEO of Duarte Design, which helps brands tell their stories in the boardroom and beyond.[4]

Telling compelling stories also causes the brain to release dopamine into the system, making it easier to remember with greater accuracy.[5] This neurotransmitter is key in triggering one of stories' biggest benefits for brand-builders—they're easily remembered. And when something is easily remembered, it's more easily shared. And your body reacts physically as well.

Stories are powerful patterns that can trigger responses both neurologically and physically on the part of the listener. They're mechanisms for communicating meaning that are easily recalled and shared. That's why they've been tools for passing on lore, morals, and values, dating back to ancient civilizations.

In short, stories work. So how do we get started with all this storytelling wizardry?

Shapes and Archetypes

Storytelling can be deceptively simple. As kids, we excel at it. We tell stories constantly. So, what happens? We grow up. We go to work. Simply put, what the millennials call "adulting" ruins us. Inhibitions take hold and we become risk-adverse. Storytelling is a right-brained behavior that we struggle with as the grown-up world nudges us further and further to the left.

What's the emerging-brand storyteller to do? First, you have to know what kind of story you're telling. As a proud Iowan, it doesn't take much to get me to share any connection to the Tall-Corn State. One story that many know already is that the academic institution where I teach, the University of Iowa, is home to the legendary Iowa Writer's Workshop, which has nurtured the talents of authors such as John Irving and Flannery O'Connor.

Another connection to the program is Kurt Vonnegut, who began his classic novel *Slaughterhouse-Five* while teaching at the Writer's Workshop (fun fact: Vonnegut's drawings in books like *Breakfast of Champions* inspired my drawings in this book). Despite his literary fame, Vonnegut called his rejected master's thesis his "prettiest contribution to culture." In it Vonnegut says that you can plot a story's arc or shape based on the ups and downs of the main character. He went on to plot various stories using some of the more common shapes such as "Man in a Hole" (Example: *The Goonies*) and "Boy Meets Girl" (Example: *Pretty Woman*).[6]

This is not to say that you should write a romantic comedy starring your business. However, Vonnegut's shapes are prominent examples of story archetypes. Archetypes are recurrent themes, common structures, or patterns (again!) that we use to tell stories based on the familiar. If the brain is hardwired for story, we can take advantage of some of the more common story shapes or archetypes to position who we are and what we stand for.

Christopher Booker makes most of us authors look like hacks. That's because he spent 34 years writing his book *The Seven Basic Plots: Why We Tell Stories*. Like Vonnegut, Booker felt that there were essential archetypes driving almost every story told. Here's an overview of five of his seven archetypes that you can apply to your brand.[7]

1. **Overcoming the Monster.** The protagonist sets out to defeat an antagonistic force (often evil), which threatens the protagonist and/or protagonist's homeland.

- *Popular examples: Star Wars: A New Hope,* the Harry Potter books and movies, and the James Bond franchise.
- *Brand examples:* Brands who adapt this story archetype are rebels. From its 1984 ad to the more literal Mac vs. PC, Apple has always fought the monster. Dollar Shave Club boldly takes on the monstrous process of "going to the store and overpaying for shave tech."[8]
- *How to use:* This story is dependent on having an antagonist. Who or what are you fighting against?

2. **Rags to Riches.** The poor protagonist acquires things such as power, wealth, and a mate, before losing it all and gaining it back upon growing as a person.

- *Popular examples: Cinderella, Rocky,* and *Aladdin.*
- *Brand examples:* These brands are often at the center of underdog stories, like Avis, who famously embraced their second-place status in the rental car industry by saying that they tried harder as a result. Scrappy founders like Paul Mitchell and Wendy's Dave Thomas also have rags to riches at the heart of their brand stories.
- *How to use:* The dynamic of "before and after" along with overall growth is key for this type of story. Where did you come from?

3. **The Quest.** The protagonist and some companions set out to acquire an important object or to get to a location, facing many obstacles and temptations along the way.

- *Popular examples: Lord of the Rings, Indiana Jones,* and *Harold & Kumar Go to White Castle.*
- *Brand examples:* Epic brands in search of something bigger are on a quest of their own. Salesforce wants to liberate users from software and connect them to their data and customers. Axe body spray wants to connect customers with others in a more . . . literal sense.
- *How to use:* An ideal that you are striving toward is key to implementing this archetype. What do you believe in? What are you and you alone on a quest to achieve?

4. **Voyage and Return.** The protagonist goes to a strange land and, after overcoming the threats it poses to him or her, returns with experience.

- *Popular examples: The Wizard of Oz, Apollo 13,* and *Finding Nemo.*
- *Brand examples:* This plot is dependent on learning something—a better way—as a result of a journey. Starbucks's Howard Schultz learned from backpacking across Europe that coffee shops in America could be more than just diners and donut shops. MagicLeap promises a better classroom experience based on their leading-edge work in augmented reality (AR).
- *How to use:* What unique experience informs your enlightened perspective? Where have you been, and what has it taught you?

5. **Rebirth.** During the course of the story, an important event forces the main characters to change their ways, often making them better people.

- *Popular examples: A Christmas Carol, How the Grinch Stole Christmas,* and the *Doctor Who* series (the Doctor regenerates as a new actor every few seasons).
- *Brand examples:* Similar to brands embracing the Voyage and Return plot, this story represents a transformation. Extreme examples include brands like Vidal Sassoon and *Vanity Fair* magazine, both of which ceased operations for years to retool before returning—reinvigorated—to the market. It can also just be striving to do something better. One-to-one brands like Tom's and Warby Parker wanted to do more than just sell shoes and glasses.
- *How to use:* Has your brand been born again? Have you undergone a reboot? How does this inform your brand's story?

The two not covered here focus more on the traditional story-telling genres of comedy and tragedy, which can certainly be applied with greater analysis. (In fact, there's more on comedy and humor in the Brand Now Toolbox.) This is a start. Do you have a clear enemy—a competitor or rival process—that you're rebelling against? You may be overcoming a monster of your own. Are you on a quest? Striving toward an ideal or trying to achieve something for your customer? Start writing your epic tale through Middle Earth.

You get the idea. Based on these common plots to common stories, you know what happens next. By finding elements of story and plot that work for your brand, you can embrace other archetypal tools.

These familiar stories help you and your audience get on the same page. For example, when a group of screenwriters at Disney pitched the movie that would eventually become *The Lion King*, studio executives were not convinced. The screenwriters pivoted their pitch, explaining that this was "Hamlet with lions." Familiar stories can help you get the job done.[9]

Now that you know what kind of story you're telling, what's involved in it? What other key ingredients does your story need?

Characters and Conflicts

Story is actually pretty simple. You have a plot. Now you need characters, conflict, and a distinctive voice. Connecting these dots is where the power of your brand story lies. The first question you have to answer is: Who is your story about? In business, we're quick to think that we're telling our own story. While your brand is certainly a factor, what you're really telling is a story about your customer or audience. As Marty Neumeier writes in *The Brand Flip*, "Your brand is a continuing story told by both the company and its customers. Every brand is a running narrative, a story-in-progress whose hero is the customer."[10]

I stumbled upon a perfect example of a customer-driven brand story while strolling through the terminal at Boston's Logan Airport where I saw a wall-sized ad featuring an Oreo cookie splashing into a big glass of milk. The headline: "Mondelēz International is reinvesting savings to grow. And guess how much we're helping them save?" That's right. This wasn't an Oreo ad. It was an ad for strategy/consulting giant Accenture featuring their client, Oreo's corporate parent Mondelēz. Accenture is embracing a "quest" story to help their customers like Mondelēz save money. As such, the featured character in the story isn't Accenture. It's their customers.

The main character isn't you. It's your customer. As we explored when we looked at meaning, get to know them and what they want. "You need your audience to be an actor in your story. Not passive listeners," stresses idea whisperer and presentation strategist Tamsen Webster.[11]

In talks that weave lessons from the Chickasaw people to Ira Glass, Bobby Lehew is an expert in storytelling. "We think we are logical and rational, so we create stories with features and benefits. In fact, we're governed by emotions," says Lehew. "Listen for what your customers aren't telling you. Listen for the interjections—the surprises and the expletives."[12] That's where you can find emotion that you can build on for your customers and character, beyond the features and benefits we too often rely on.

Now that you know who the main character is, what happens next? In classic storytelling, you have your protagonist. What you need is an antagonist. Lest you think your brand needs a mustache-twirling 19th-century villain, let me remind you that an antagonist is anything—a character, group of characters, institution, or concept—that presents or represents opposition to the protagonist. Many of the common story plots depend on an antagonist ("Overcoming the Monster" is defined by it).

What is your audience struggling with? What challenges stand in their way? Mac has the PC. Starbucks has regular ol' drip coffee—or anything that seeks to make coffee unremarkable. Your point has a counterpoint, and it's important to paint that picture as you tell your story. Plus, your antagonist sets off other plot points that will help your story stand out to your audience.

Many organizations focus on minimizing conflict in their communications, rounding out the rough edges in their stories. But conflict is good. In fact, it's central to Patagonia's story. As counterintuitive as it may seem, as a sustainably minded clothing company, Patagonia actively encourages customers *not* to buy new jackets if there's nothing wrong with the one they have. Take a moment and think about that last sentence. Who in commerce does this? Most approach current customers as people you can sell more to. Not Patagonia. They'll even help you mend your coat if it's damaged.

This rebirth story (we can do better, we can be better) does a few things. First, the push-pull, the inner-struggle of the company being both active in manufacturing and commerce and understanding their environmental impact, is interesting. This conflict creates contrast and helps Patagonia stand out in the crowded outerwear market. Finally, Patagonia's story also empowers their customers to do better, making them a part of the ongoing brand story as well.

We know what the plot is. We know who's involved (characters) and what they're up against (conflict). But what about the voice? How do you actually tell the story?

Say It with Voice

Remember, it's not what you say: it's how you say it. This ancient proverb has served as a constant reminder that it's as much about the medium as it is the message. This is as true as ever today. Media has changed—and continues to change—rapidly. However, it remains a tool for telling our stories, and it's a tool that is dependent on voice.

We create meaning, structure, and story. We convey all this with a distinct voice. Or at least we should be doing that. As media has evolved and gotten more complex, we're responding the best we can. We work to keep up with the latest social networks, creating the newest forms of content, but we often forget to create a distinct brand voice.

How distinct is your voice? "Try the logo test," says Ann Handley, Chief Content Officer at MarketingProfs and best-selling author of *Everybody Writes*. "If your logo or label was masked, would your customers know it's your content and not your competition's?"[13] Think about your own content. Would it pass this test? If your hope is to create a standout brand, one of the best tools for communicating this is a distinct voice.

The first headquarters of the Duluth Trading Company was a refurbished barge on the waterfront of Lake Superior in the downtown shipping district of Duluth, Minnesota. It was there that two brothers who described themselves as "woolly, hippie tradesmen kinda guys" started making utilitarian products for their fellow workers. Bucket organizers, long-tail shirts (to prevent the epidemic of plumber's butt), and more. "Anything that will help guys in the trades work smarter, work more comfortably, we're out to develop."[14] And they don't just create products. They share stories with a distinct voice.

One of Duluth Trading Company's best sellers is Buck Naked Underwear, a product name infused with brand voice whose tagline promises that it "feels like wearing nothing at all. No pinch, no stink, no sweat." Another pair of organic cotton underwear will "give your rooster a comfortable booster."[15]

Duluth Trading Company isn't leaving much to the imagination. But it's a memorable story. A quest plot (helping guys in the trades work) expressed in the descriptive albeit blunt language of those they serve. The main characters are the workers who find salvation from their challenges (pinch, stink, sweat) in the form of underwear from Duluth Trading Company.

Don't make the mistake of editing yourself for fear of offending others. Especially when those others might not be your core customers. BarkBox was looking for ways to flesh out their social media editorial calendar with more playful content. #Throwback-Thursday and other themed days are the norm, so why wouldn't you celebrate Wednesday, or "hump day," as it's called in some circles? And if you were observing "hump day" and were in the dog business in a very fun way, maybe you would do so by posting photos of . . . dogs. Humping. Want proof? Check out stories.barkpost.com/literally-hump-day/.

It's a lot of fun, and it fits their brand. But it wasn't a no-brainer. As BarkBox cofounder Henrik Werdelin explained, "We would post all these pictures, and there were people who got upset. Our viewpoint was a little bit, well yes, you might alienate some people, but to be honest, this is what we find very funny, and if we find it very funny, then we bet there are a lot of other people who think it's very funny, so we should just be doing that. Then the people who like us, who like this kind of silly humor will gravitate to us, too."[16]

A distinct voice conveys meaning and story. So how do you go about creating one? You have to start by determining what aspects are most demonstrative to your brand's personality. For example, Whole Foods has a distinct voice that is communicated through a variety of touchpoints, both online and in-store. "Our voice and tone guidelines set visual, storytelling, and copy parameters across channels. Our content pillars—Food Adventure, Real Wellness, and Local & Fresh—serve as the foundation of our content strategy and storytelling approach across channels," says Lisa Grimm, Integrated Brand Content and Social Media Director at Whole Foods.

This specific, digestible document is then shared with each of the Whole Foods channel owners so that they can adapt it based on the format of the network. "For example, our Instagram voice is different from our Facebook voice is different from our Pinterest voice, so on and so forth. Hashtags like #eattherainbow and #delish are critical in Instagram, whereas they're irrelevant elsewhere," adds Grimm.[17]

Uberflip, a content marketing platform, takes things a step further. Their style guide is not only shared internally, it's a public page online—anyone can see it (styleguide.uberflip.com). Like Whole Foods, they have a section on brand voice, titled "How to talk like an Uberflipper." On it, they use the following adjectives to describe their brand:[18]

→ Cheeky, but not offensive
→ Accessible, but not fluffy
→ Progressive, but not aloof

Another thing Uberflip is doing right? Their voice specifies what they are, as well as what they aren't. Remember, antagonists can be good. Conflict creates contrast, and contrast helps you stand out.

While attitudes and emotions can be effective descriptors of brand voice, make sure they are actionable and audience focused. Poo~Pourri knows a thing or two about brand personality. The innovative bathroom spray is the brainchild of essential oils expert Suzy Batiz, who founded the company based on a dare to "trap bathroom odor" from her husband and brother. After a year of fragrant experimentation, she managed to do this using her oils.

In telling the story, Batiz knew that "natural" was simply a feature. While Poo~Pourri products are all natural, that's not the only definition of the brand. "It's one of the characteristics of the brand, but you can't bank your whole business on that. You have to go back and personify, humanize your brand," says Batiz.[19] This is a pretty revolutionary idea—especially in the natural-products category—and one that's overlooked by many.

"I had to use humor," adds Batiz. "Think about it. We only tell fart and poop jokes to our close family."[20] Why is this? It builds closeness and familiarity, yet another example of stories and voice connecting and creating meaning. Poo~Pourri's humorous voice is present across every brand touchpoint, especially their innovative packaging. Understanding voice also helps Poo~Pourri maintain consistency. "It would be easy to forget about 'her,'" Batiz shares, noting that the Poo~Pourri brand is personified internally as "her." That's because Batiz knew that the brand should be "beautiful and feminine."[21] This brand personification has been brought to life recently in a series of online videos.

Personifying your brand voice doesn't have to be this elaborate, either. Sometimes it's as simple as a shift in tense. As a government agency, NASA recognized that Twitter was a cost-effective way for keeping the public informed on the travels of their rovers exploring Mars. When tweeting for the Curiosity Rover (@MarsCuriosity on Twitter), NASA's social media manager, Veronica McGregor, realized that she could save characters by substituting "I traveled" for phrases such as "the spacecraft has traveled."[22] This had the surprising effect of personifying what was essentially a piece of machinery, transforming third-person reports from the rover into first-person stories. From there, they began to experiment with occasional pop culture references and song lyrics.

This, too, is a quest plot (um, going to freaking Mars!) with all of us watching and the rover sharing, using humor to add impact. The result of this story is a greater connection to scientific exploration and discovery—the very heart of NASA's mission. And the very heart of brand personification, which is key in conveying a compelling story.

Layering Your Story

So, now that you have a story—grounded with meaning, structure, characters, conflict, and voice—what do you do? Where does this story live?

When I talk through all this in the classroom and at conferences and events, this is where, after everyone spends a few minutes nodding along, someone slowly raises a hand to ask, "So . . . is this like . . . your slogan? Or . . . is it like . . . a thirty-second ad? Or . . . is it like . . . what you're supposed to say and do on social media?" Quick answers—Yes, yes, and yes.

Of course, story as a framework is incredibly big and infinitely applicable. As a brand, you have several places that you're telling stories. From digital and broadcast media to offline, in-person experiences. Your stories infuse them all. Now how about a less-abstract answer?

Your story has layers. Like an onion, you keep peeling and eventually you find the core. For your brand, that's your core story. This is at the heart of everything you do. It's built on the meaning established earlier and supported by the structural elements in this chapter and the previous one. Your core story may be something that you can distill into a brand promise, but that may be asking a lot.

Your core story, like Vonnegut's shapes and Booker's plots, is an archetype that you can use everywhere. The rebirth plot is central to the Method brand, which promises better cleaning and better cleaning products. This is a part of their packaging, advertising, and the content they share online. Your core story ripples out throughout the rest of your brand touchpoints.

Speaking of the stories we share online, what about . . . those other stories. Those upper-case Stories we find on Facebook, Instagram, and Snapchat. This, my friends, is the hardest part of writing a book about media and technology. Inevitably, as hard as you try, you miss something. Before the ink is dry, Facebook crashes and burns (doubtful). Or they finally buy Snapchat (instead of trying to emulate it) and finally form SnapFace. Regardless, I try to remain somewhat channel-agnostic. Or, when making a reference, I try to use the low-hanging fruit like those mentioned previously.

But Stories—collages of short photos and videos tricked out with emojis, colorful scribbles, and animated effects that disappear after a 24-hour time period—are increasingly popular features on most major social networks. Is your story something that can help you create Stories? In keeping with my previous theme of concise answers—yes. Furthermore, I think these concise stories can help you think through and apply some of the structural elements of story and voice discussed here.

Chickasaw storyteller Mary Frances Thompson, best known as Te Ata, once said: "Stories are like this old ragweed. They all come from the same root, but they spread out, this way, that way."[23] One of the biggest ways that our stories spread today is through online content.

BUILDING BLOCKS

- What is your brand's core story? Think of the common story plots outlined in this chapter—overcoming the monster, rags to riches, the quest, voyage and return, and rebirth. Does one of these fit you?

- Still stuck? Try answering this question: If your brand was a movie, which movie would it be? What type of movie or genre is it? What kind of plot does it have? (Tip: Have a few people answer this question internally—you should see themes emerge.)

- Do you have a distinct brand voice? Try Ann Handley's cover-the-logo test. Does this sound like you and you alone, or could it be anyone?

- Need another brand-voice tip? If you were to cast an actor or actress to play your brand, who would it be? What does that tell you about the qualities of your brand voice?

- How can you share your story and voice internally? Can you make a style guide like Whole Foods? Again, Uberflip has a great style guide that's online for everyone to see. Find it at styleguide.uberflip.com.

FOUR
Content

It's a blustery day on a frozen lake in Albert Lea, Minnesota. A hovercraft roars up across the center of the lake in front of three deer—a male and two does—stranded on the ice, legs spread-eagled. "They just can't get up and go, can they?" says one snowsuit-clad man to another. The deer are trapped on the slick frozen surface. "She's [referring to a specific doe] probably tired—probably been out here a couple of days."

After weighing their options, the men grab some rope, tie a slip-knot, which they place around a deer. "Get ready for a ride, Bambi!" they announce as they pull the deer across the lake and back to the shore. "Well, let's go get her sister." They return, pulling the sister back to land. They continue until all three deer have been pulled to the shore. The first doe rises on her tired shaky legs and eventually hops back into the woods. Cut to a wide shot of the lake as the following text fades in:

"James and his father saved three deer that day . . . After some rest, all three returned to the forest."

I don't know James or his father. They made this video using their GoPro camera. GoPro found it, added some soaring instrumental music, and made it their video of the day. It has nearly eight million views now.[1] I found it a few years ago and show it in my class as an example of effective content marketing. I've watched it all the way through more times that I can count.

And I damn near cry every time.

It's a beautiful video with a moving story. It's a hero's story. I'm not making an inference here. GoPro says this at the end, on the single branded card they put up with their logo and the line "Be a Hero." If you want to, you can categorize this as an ad for an electronics company. But I think it's something bigger.

It's a great story, told effectively through content. Unless you've been hiding under a rock, you've probably heard a thing or two about content marketing. Google's Eric Schmidt famously noted that "every two days, we create as much information online as we did from the dawn of civilization up until 2003."[2] People are hungry for information. And not just for learning. Google's data also shows us that the average consumer is now seeking out twice as much content in making their purchase decisions as they were just a few short years ago.

Now that you know your brand's story, it's time to move it. And the single greatest tool for moving your story is content. To break this down, we'll explore what makes good content, how the layers of your story become levels of your content, and we'll examine the question on every marketer's mind—how much content is enough? There's also a secret tool at the end as well.

First, let's look a bit deeper at the double-edged sword that is content marketing.

The Trouble with Content

It used to be so easy: if you had a strong enough brand and an okay story, you could step up to the traditional media megaphone and broadcast your message to the masses. I'll spare you the marketing-disruption lecture and simply say—it doesn't work like that anymore.

On one hand, this is great. New technology in the form of social networks, content, email, and more allows the brand to be in control of media and reach. It's less dependent (but not totally independent) on budget and other resources. GoPro didn't need a media budget to share their video with the masses: they uploaded it to YouTube, and the Internet took care of the rest.

To channel Tevye from *Fiddler on the Roof*, on the other hand . . .

 This is not so great. Not because everything just mentioned isn't a positive development: it's that it's now harder than ever before. It's harder to keep track of—new social networks, new features, new features on new social networks, new forms of content, new forms of advertising. As I said in *Get Scrappy,* with all these shiny new things it's easy for marketers to fall prey to checklist marketing. Blindly checking channels off of an arbitrary list. It's the same with content.

No one is going to tell you that content doesn't matter. Whether it's in the latest digital marketing trends or from the keynote at an industry event, we're constantly being told that "content is king" and that we must "think like a publisher" if we want to stand out online today.

It's easy to nod along, roll up our sleeves, and dive headfirst into the content-marketing business. In the beginning, it feels great. We're creating! Publishing blog posts, videos, podcasts, ebooks, infographics, and more. At the end of the day, there's something there now that wasn't there before as a result of our hard work. It feels like we're "doing digital marketing correctly." *That content thing that the best practices article talked about?? We do a ton of that!*

It's not just you. We've all fallen head over heels for content marketing. According to the latest data from the Content Marketing Institute and MarketingProfs, 88 percent of marketers use content marketing, with 76 percent noting that they're on track to produce more content this year versus last year.[3]

But more isn't always better. Nor is it particularly effective. While content-production levels are soaring, the same data from the Content Marketing Institute/MarketingProfs also shows that only 30 percent of B2B marketers say their organizations are effective at content marketing, down from 38 percent last year.[4]

This aligns with a larger concern presented by marketing consultant, educator, and author Mark W. Schaefer. In his book *The Content Code*, Schaefer outlines a dynamic called "content shock."[5] As the amount of information online continues to grow—thanks to all us content creators—it will be harder and harder to stand out. We'll be creating more content than there will be people to consume it. In short, content is creating one of the noisiest marketplaces ever in the history of commerce.

Simply producing more content isn't enough, as you'll soon discover. You have to create *better* content. How does one do that? By creating content that is both business-centric and customer-aware.

Grounded In Strategy

The first step is admitting you have a problem. You can't create content just for the sake of doing so. If this seems far-fetched, ask yourself—have you ever wanted to start some new effort just because it sounded cool? Or because your competitor just launched one?

So why should you create content, then? Content is a tool for sharing your brand's story. Communicating your meaning. What you're all about. Content can help you do many things. It can help you:

→ Move your stories online and off
→ Develop your audience
→ Position your expertise
→ Deliver value to your customers
→ Solve problems for your customers
→ And much, much more

While content can be infinitely useful, don't let its utility prevent you from being specific. Let's take a look at one more stat from the Content Marketing Institute and MarketingProfs. While we're producing more content than ever, fewer marketers have a documented content-marketing strategy compared with last year (32 percent vs. 35 percent), even though the same research consistently shows that those who document their strategy are more effective in nearly all areas of content marketing.[6]

You have to ground the content that you're creating not only in who you are as a brand, but in what you want your customers to do. What purpose does this content serve? If you're treading into new and innovative territory, you may need to paint a vivid picture of what it is you're trying to do.

Most know Watson as the question-answering computer developed by IBM that defeated *Jeopardy!* champions Brad Rutter and Ken Jennings in 2011. (Ken Jennings? Another Iowan.) Since then, Big Blue has been focused on putting Watson's machine learning to work for brands, "understanding the questions that humans ask and providing answers." Watson has been used by brands such as 1-800-Flowers, *Bon Appétit*, and H&R Block. I'll be honest, even reading my own brief overview of this, my response is, "Okay . . . cool . . . but . . . um, how?"

The IBM Watson Group has a strategic need to communicate how Watson is impacting businesses. Enter the Watson blog (ibm.com/blogs/watson/). With post titles such as "5 things you need to know about the future of messaging platforms" and "Customer analytics in the time of bots," this is more than just content for the sake of content. It's content demonstrating expertise and sharing stories at the bleeding edge of artificial intelligence and customer analytics.

And your strategic grounding doesn't have to be as complex as machine learning. Sometimes it can be as simple as providing customers with peace of mind. Lucky Pawz in Iowa City is a dog daycare and boarding center that uses their blog to offer pet parents just that. Their daily posts showcase photos of pups at play. Like IBM, Lucky Pawz is blogging for a very specific reason.

Both brands have something else in common, too. While both accomplish very specific business objectives, they also share the other key ingredient in creating standout content: both are focused on their customers.

Customer-First Content

Effective, standout content is both business-centric and customer-aware. You need to look at what purpose your content serves, but you also need to consider who it's for. What are their needs? "Brands that we look to, that are charismatic, know their audience. They know who they are," says Carla Johnson, coauthor of *Experiences: The 7th Era of Marketing.* "When you tell a story driven by empathy, you'll always see results."[7]

Empathy is critical in creating customer-focused standout content. What kind of complex research do you need to undertake in order to learn more about what matters to your customers? "Just talk to them," adds Johnson.[8] So, what do you talk about? Start with a simple question.

Marcus Sheridan, of River Pools and Spas and the consulting business The Sales Lion, rebuilt his pool empire through the power of questions. His story has been documented far and wide. When I interviewed him on my podcast, I asked him for the twenty-second version of his story. "In 2008, I was going to lose my business. I had two consultants tell me to file for bankruptcy. I started reading about inbound marketing and content marketing and created a four-word philosophy: They ask, you answer."[9] (This philosophy is also the title of Sheridan's book.) And the rest is history.

Sheridan set out with the simple strategy of answering his customers' questions. *How much should a pool cost? Variable-speed pool pumps vs. one- and two-speed, which is best?* These questions inspired content (both are actual River Pools blog post titles). These questions are also connected to customer needs and focused on a business objective.

As an irreverent men's grooming company, Dollar Shave Club uses their blog to answer men's questions about everything from grooming ("What's that stuff in my belly button?") and health

("How much muscle can you gain in 90 days?"). None of this content is hard-sell or product-focused. It's lifestyle content that means something to their customers. Dollar Shave Club also provides a worthwhile reminder that not all effective content is online. While digital content is more cost-effective, there are moments in the overall brand experience where a hard copy is better. Enter Dollar Shave Club's newsletter, "Bathroom Minutes," their highly portable publication meant for reading while you're indisposed. As the masthead notes, the helpful articles are "Time Well Spent."

Sick of being stung and having to spend a whole week harvesting honey, Australian father-and-son beekeepers Stu and Cedar Anderson set out to change beekeeping for the better. Their innovative Flow Hive transforms the box into a system for providing fresh honey on tap. I'm going to level with you, beekeeping is an endeavor I would have a lot of questions about. Flow Hive knows this, too, which is why their videos answer each and every question an amateur beekeeper would have, from "How to grow food for your bees" to "How to protect your Flow Hive from bears." Geez. I thought the bees were crazy enough: now we have *bears* in the equation?!? I have not missed my calling. I'll stick to branding and marketing, thank you very much.

Your customers should be the heroes of your story. As such, they can also serve as the stars of your content as well. IBM Watson Group uses their blog to share stories from customers such as Tesla, Woodside Energy, and Walmart. The GoPro video with the deer rescue that makes me ugly cry—er, is very moving—wasn't a one-off for the camera company. Their entire content strategy is focused on sharing their customers' stories, from snowboarding to a five-year-old "Mini Bruce Lee."

Content that shares your customers' stories ultimately ends up sharing *your* stories. Your content should be designed for your customer. That's why it's better in the long run to be a content brand, rather than just another company creating branded content. This could sound like hair-splitting, but it's a set of semantic hoops that are worth jumping through. Branded content has been around forever. And it's not usually pretty. It's often defined by sterile white papers and polished corporate blogs. The information may be useful from a business perspective, but it's not engaging from the audience's perspective. And remember, the audience isn't you or your company. "Content brands are created for an audience, while branded content is created for a business," says Andrew Davis, author of *Brandscaping* and *Town Inc.* "A content brand creates an actual asset."[10]

You need to focus on creating content brands that people want to hear from. To many, Content Marketing Institute Founder Joe Pulizzi is the father of modern content marketing. As the author of *Epic Content Marketing* and *Content Inc.*, as well as being the organizer of the largest content-marketing event in the world, Content Marketing World, I'd say this is true. (He also produced an amazing documentary on content marketing, which I reference in "Further Reading and Resources.")

"Content marketing is old," says Pulizzi. While there's been a renaissance recently, it dates back to Benjamin Franklin using *Poor Richard's Almanac* as an engine for generating print sales. With *Poor Richard*, Franklin created a content brand. Likewise, John Deere followed suit with their farming magazine *The Furrow*. It wasn't called John Deere Magazine. Indeed, most readers struggle to connect the brand back to its parent company. "Look at Adobe," says Pulizzi. "It's not the Adobe blog. It's CMO.com."[11]

Patagonia has several content brands including their blog the Cleanest Line and their Worn Wear blog, the previously mentioned online knowledge base for helping customers repair their clothes so they don't have to replace them hastily. One of the most prominent examples of a content brand is Blendtec. The company sells what can only be described as weapons-grade blenders for commercial kitchens. Blendtec's content strategy is as unique as their product. Instead of setting up a booth at a commercial kitchen trade show, a happy accident occurred when the marketing director spotted founder Tom Dickson using their blender to blend matches around the office. From these humble experiments, their video series *Will It Blend?* was born. The videos are a joy to watch. Dickson brings a child's delight along with a game-show aesthetic as he blends every-thing from golf balls and iPhones to an entire Thanksgiving dinner. As of July 2017, the Blendtec series of videos has garnered more than 283 million views on YouTube.[12]

The videos are so much fun, it's easy to miss the best practices at play. First, the content is business-centric. They have a high-end product that they need to demo. Second, it's customer-aware. With all the noise in the marketplace today, who wants to watch someone show off a new product? They could have told you about the metal in the blades or about the power of the engine, but I'll bet you'd have lost interest by then. They found an engaging story shape—the game show—to apply to their content marketing challenge.

Finally, instead of calling it Blendtec Blends or something else heavily branded and easily forgettable, they created a content brand in *Will It Blend*? And a content brand with a question in its name. How's that for a content marketing home run?

How Much Content Should You Create?

Speaking of questions, I'm sure this section's heading represents a big question that's on your mind. In breaking down the content-crowded digital ecosystem, you may have noticed a theme emerging. It's one I started in *Get Scrappy*. If you're a brand builder with limited resources, the last thing you should be trying to do is everything. Especially if it's using all the channels and creating all the content for no reason at all.

While *Get Scrappy* was about resource limitations, *Brand Now* is about building a better brand. In working through the seven dynamics, this has come into focus by creating meaning, adding structure, and refining the stories that we share through our content. Unless it fits your brand's framework like a glove—from the dual perspective of both your business and your customers—don't do it.

I'll say that last part again. If there's no reason for creating this content, for the love of God, please don't. As Doug Kessler, cofounder and creative director of the London-based B2B content marketing agency Velocity Partners, quipped, "The biggest threat to content marketing is content marketing." Heed Doug's advice. Don't be a part of the problem by creating more me-too content. "Every piece you put out can either help or hurt your brand," adds Kessler, going on to say that you should never create so much content that it interferes with your overall quality.[13]

Sometimes creating more content is strategic. Using customer-centricity as your guide, there are times when the layers of your story make logical levels of content. Sometimes your audience doesn't want the whole story at once. This makes me think of the CIA, Julia Child, and Shark Week.

Did I lose you? I'll back up. You may be surprised to learn that the CIA—yes, the Central Intelligence Agency—has a pretty powerful social media and content marketing strategy. In addition to a coy brand voice cleverly designed to warm the public to our national spy agency, the content they share is also very topical. For example, during the Discovery Channel's annual Shark Week in 2015, the CIA provided a perfect blueprint for content leveling.

The whole story was powered by the fun fact that Julia Child—yes, *that* Julia Child—spent time during World War II developing a recipe for shark repellent for the Office of Strategic Services, the predecessor of the CIA. They started with a small, fun piece of content for the masses. A tweet with the fact, a link to the recipe, and a fun animated GIF of Julia herself chopping shark meat. This link took you to a story on their blog about the shark repellent. From there, those curious could read a longer story on Julia Child's life prior to her French cuisine fame.[14]

The CIA leveled their content based on the varied interest levels of their audience. It can help to think of your audience as swimmers with various levels of experience. You need to create content for skimmers (those dangling their feet only), swimmers (average interest), and divers (deep interest and expertise).

Organizing and leveling content requires complex skills. While we need content strategists and content creators, don't forget to empower content editors as well. "Most writers are not great editors," says Ann Handley, author of *Everybody Writes* and *Content Rules*.

"The value of the editor cannot be understated. The editor is the proxy for the audience."[15]

How can brands "up" their editing game? "Peer editing is a great start," continues Handley. "There's also the Hemingway Editor app and Grammarly."[16] As it turns out, more brands and bloggers are turning to editors—with one in four having a formal process in place for editing, as reported in a survey from Orbit Media.[17] "Most content marketing is stuck in the 'meh' gear," says Robert Rose, Chief Strategist for the Content Advisory Group with the Content Marketing Institute and coauthor of *Experiences: The 7th Era of Marketing*.[18] And most of this "meh content" is due to the fact that we lack focus—both strategically and with what our customers want. In many cases we're creating too much content. Editing—both the strategy and the content itself—can help with that.

There's one more thing that can help your brand's content.

A Content Marketing Secret: Don't Hate It

In addition to being a great actor, Alec Baldwin is also an exceptional podcast host. On his show *Here's the Thing,* he has in-depth conversations with legends like David Letterman and trendsetters like Lena Dunham. However, it was during an interview with public radio's Ira Glass where I uncovered a secret tool for improving your brand's content.

Toward the end of the show, Baldwin asked Glass what he saw himself doing next—when *This American Life* and other Glass-led ventures such as *Serial* eventually come to an end. His answer? "I don't know. . . . I really like making stuff." He then stated that he intended to create, produce, and edit audio for as long as he possibly could.[19] Why? Because he genuinely likes doing it.

With more and more brands in the content-creation business, it's easy to overanalyze the task. It's easy to over-plan in an attempt to construct a perfectly crafted masterpiece that fits your audience like a glove. While your community's needs are indeed paramount, in planning for them we sometimes fail to account for another key constituency.

You.

You will be the one living with this content. You will be the one responsible for every aspect of its creation, production, and promotion. You will know every piece of it inside and out. And yet we often fail to account for our personal strengths and weaknesses when mapping out our content strategies.

Not so with Dave Gerhardt, director of marketing at Drift, a Boston-based start-up that helps sales teams connect with their customers. When he was a guest on my podcast, I asked how he created standout content. "My approach is simple," he said. "I create content that I would like. There's no sexy playbook."[20] From Dollar Shave Club to BarkBox, many of the brands in this book embrace this approach. If it's something they like—and that they think their people will like—they trust their gut and do it.

When leading one of my Content Marketing Boot Camps, I close with a similar theme. You don't have to like the content-creation process—but it sure helps. What do I mean? I mean that if it's between writing blog posts and creating a video series, you should start with the form that you are most passionate about. If writing comes more easily for you and you are horrified at the idea of creating and editing video, start with what you like. Think of it as crawling to walk.

That's not to say that you shouldn't try creating anything outside of your comfort zone. However, the core of your content marketing engine should be a task that you like. In addition to helping with your sanity, this bit of advice is also strategic, as it helps to ensure that your content marketing is sustainable. When you like creating your content, you'll create more of it and it'll be harder for you to fall off the wagon.

This approach also guarantees the presence of another often-elusive key ingredient to good content—heart. When you like what you do, that extra bit of care gets baked into what you create. Go listen to Ira Glass's work, and you can tell he cares about what he does and enjoys doing it. The same is true of good content from marketers who care.

With a content-marketing plan in place—one that is centered on both your business and your audience—you're ready to share your brand's story. But who will help you do all this? The answer lies ahead.

BUILDING BLOCKS

- There's too much content! What kind of content can your brand create that no one else can?

- Where in the buyer's journey is there a problem? A disconnect? Can you create content to help alleviate that?

- Are there questions your customers have that you can be answering with your content?

- Are you creating too much content? Try focusing on one piece of content and seeing if you can add levels for "skimmers, swimmers, and divers."

- Do you have a plan in place for editing your content? If not, where could you start?

- If there were no other factors involved, what kind of content would you most like to create? How can you build on that?

FIVE
Community

If you were to go through my personal effects, among them you'd find the following: blueprints for the Starship *Enterprise*, two Starfleet uniforms (my wife insists on calling them "costumes" but whatever), autographs from William Shatner and James Doohan, and a Klingon Dictionary.

Yes, I am a Star Trek fan. A Trekker, as we prefer to be called (don't make the mistake of calling a fan a "Trekkie"). I was in peak fandom at the age of thirteen. Old enough to hang out with my friends (also Trek fans), but not really old enough to go anywhere, we spent Friday night sleepovers daisy-chaining VCRs together so that we could record our own personal copies of the original 79 episodes of *Star Trek*. I've told you before that I'm very cool, right?

Fans have been important to the life and longevity of Star Trek. Fans literally saved the original series from cancellation, which brought us the third season. We wouldn't have had classic, kooky episodes like "Spock's Brain" if it hadn't been for the letter-writing campaign initiated by superfan Bjo Trimble. Her fandom and dedication didn't end there. Trimble and her husband also helped with the campaign to have the first of NASA's space shuttles named *Enterprise*, efforts that were rewarded with uncredited roles as crew members in *Star Trek: The Motion Picture*.[1]

Why does everyone care about this science fiction franchise so much? In a lot of ways, Star Trek got me through the truly awful and awkward parts of adolescence. And while it may not be my first, it's definitely one of the strongest fan groups I've ever been a part of. As any nerd will tell you, when you don't fit in in other traditional settings, connecting with your people over a shared topic is huge. That's why—corny as it may sound—Star Trek conventions are so very important. They reinforce this sense of community. When meaning is created, people want to join. They want to be a part of it. When compelling stories are told, they gather and connect with each other.

Which brings us back to your brand. You may not be exploring strange new worlds and seeking out new life and new civilizations; but if you want your brand to boldly go where no brand has gone before, you, like Star Trek, need to embrace your fans and foster that same sense of community.

To do this, think of the Starship *Enterprise* orbiting a planet. These concentric circles will serve as a guide, while we explore the people who make up your brand's community and what you can do to engage them.

Branding in Circles

When I'm not consulting, teaching, or watching *Star Trek*, I get to do one of my other favorite things—speaking to large groups of marketers and business owners eager to build their brands and grow their businesses. People always ask, "What is one of the most unique groups you've spoken to?" I always point to the International Roller Skating Association. Beyond the amazing fact that there is a lively and exuberant professional association for rink owners, this group was also memorable for a question an audience member asked during the Q&A that followed my keynote. It was the million-dollar question: "What's one thing you would do if you were us?"

For all the other reasons discussed throughout this book—from media shifts to technology disruptions—we're all overwhelmed today. As such, we struggle to identify the actionable insights. The nuggets that we can implement right away to help improve our businesses. That's why this question is the million-dollar question.

My answer? Don't waste your time focusing on the wrong people. To fix this, you have to work your circles. Imagine all the people related to your business organized into concentric circles. Starting in the center, you have your employees. These are the people who make your business what it is. The next circle out are your business partners, vendors, distributors, and others who are a part of what your brand does but aren't on your payroll.

Working toward the outer circles, you have your customers. Remember, not all customers are equal. In your first outer circle, you have your best customers—your raving fans. Next, you have the majority of your happy customers, followed by a smaller group of transactional customers. These are the people who buy only occasionally. Finally, your big outer circle is made up of prospects. These are people who should be your customers, but aren't for whatever reason.

In outlining these groups, they're really nothing special. You've heard of these groups and may even have some specific strategies for engaging them. What you probably don't have is a system for whom to focus on and when. That's because too many of us focus only on that outer circle of prospects. Or, worse still, the general public.

Thinking of the groups that make up your brand's community in concentric circles provides an actionable strategy for engaging your fans, advocates, and ambassadors. You have to prioritize. Let's start with the most important circle and brand from the inside out.

Inside Out: Starting with Your People

This circle is literally your inner circle: your employees. These are the people who know you and your brand better than anyone else. They're in your business day in and day out. In many cases, their service and craftsmanship makes your brand what it is. This inner circle holds tremendous potential.

As Danielle Burke, VP of Product and Strategy at JobBase, writes, "Only eight percent of most employees' social networks overlap with their company's social networks and, on average, employees collectively have ten times more connections than the company brand does. When employees share information on social media, their posts go 561 percent farther than corporate posts. Brand messages distributed by employees are re-shared 24 times more often than if they come straight from the brand."[2]

Your people—your employees and their friends, family, and social connections—are some of your greatest marketing assets. And they too often go unused. (And, yes, I include your employees' family and friends. As marketers, we have to be shameless and call in favors and ask your team to do the same from time to time. Your family and friends are usually willing to help if you simply ask. Just don't go to the well too often.)

Think of the potential social graph this creates if each and every one of them is able to be an advocate for your brand. When you consider all this, engaging employees on behalf of your brand should be a no-brainer. What are we doing wrong?

To be a part of your brand and ultimately a brand ambassador, your team needs to understand your brand. Your meaning and your story. Spoiler alert: chances are they don't. According to the *Harvard Business Review*, on average only 5 percent of employees understand their company's overall strategy.[3]

Step one has to be making sure they understand who you are and what you're all about. We often think that those who excel at certain skills do so magically. That they're talented naturals. But even corporate-culture rock stars have to work hard to communicate this internally. Zappos distills their unique culture into a 352-page hardback culture book, which they update regularly and distribute to employees. The book includes core values such as "Create fun and a little weird-  ness," and "Build a positive team and a family spirit." Most of the pages, though, are dedicated to quotes from real employees about working at Zappos and what it means. "Our culture is a way of life and it has become a part of who I am," says Stacy H., while Stephanie B. notes, "I love working for a company that lets me be myself :)."[4]

"Our number one priority is company culture," says Zappos cofounder and CEO Tony Hsieh. "Our whole belief is that if you get the culture right, most of the other stuff like delivering great customer service or building a big long-term brand will just happen naturally on its own."[5]

Organizationally, most are in the habit of sharing sales data and keeping everyone updated on the latest HR policies, but we seldom make any effort to communicate our meaning to those who it matters most to. And, again, as this group is often making the product or delivering the service that is your brand, they'll probably do so better with a clearer understanding of who you are and what your story is. Happy employees who are aligned with your mission and what you stand for ultimately create a better brand experience, which creates more loyal, happy customers, Altimeter Group reports.[6]

Coldwell Banker adds an interesting layer of complexity. Their licensed real-estate professionals are the face of their brand. However, these 87,000 realtors are independent. They aren't employed by Coldwell Banker. "When you don't make a product, everyone has to be able to articulate your brand value—the 'why.' People today are so quick to jump to the 'what'," says Sean Blankenship, former Chief Marketing Officer at Coldwell Banker. "Our story is our most prized asset."[7]

How do you keep everyone on the same page while building a standout brand? "It's challenging. We don't tell them how to run their businesses (as they're independent), but we do give them a system—a brand—so they can focus on building their image at the local level."[8] In addition to the standard branded collateral, their brokers have access to a 109-page brand storybook. Like the Zappos Culture Book, this paperback book includes core values, company history, leadership, and some of their key go-to market principles.

When you open the book, you find a two-page spread featuring a photo of two young girls playing in a yard. The headline states:

"Home is more than what we sell. Home is who we are." These values were born out of the company's founding by Colbert Coldwell in the wake of the San Francisco earthquake of 1906. When many profited then at the expense of undervalued properties and vulnerable sellers, Coldwell stood on principle. Values mean even more when there's a story to back them up. As you'll recall, one of the biggest benefits of story is that it's easy to remember and share. That's why Coldwell Banker puts this story of "110 years of unwavering commitment to ethics and innovation" in the hands of their realtors.[9]

If creating a book like Coldwell Banker and Zappos sounds intimidating, try another format. Jen Slaski is the former Executive Director of Marketing Communications at Spiceworks, a support community for IT professionals. In drafting an internal brand book, she found it "hard to capture a human brand on paper" without its feeling like corporate guidelines. Thus the Spiceworks brand camp was born. "Sometime during an employee's first two months, they go to brand camp and get training on how to be the brand and bring the brand to life—how to write in the brand's voice. Our CEO called it 'corporate rehab' as it's a mindset unfamiliar to many, especially in IT. Ultimately the brand book had its place as a reference after brand camp."[10]

Storied bourbon brand Maker's Mark employs a similar approach. As a family business, it's important that all employees understand the history and traditions of founder Bill Samuels Sr. That's why his son, current Chairman Emeritus Bill Samuels Jr., hired agency professional Jim Lindsey. "We wanted to extract from my dad how he felt his brand should be positioned in the marketplace," Samuels Jr. shared with me during an interview.[11]

Instead of asking his father to describe the brand, they asked him how his friends would describe him, "as we knew the product he created was his baby." This helped capture insights on Maker's Mark's brand personality (genteel, tenacious, humorous, honest, respectful, loyal), target market ("Those with an above-average interest in taste and taste distinctiveness who we would enjoy having over for dinner"), communications strategy ("We shall not invade the airspace of others until we are invited into that airspace"), and more. They then distilled this into a presentation that all employees receive once hired. "Everyone gets a big dose of culture up front." A story told in the words of the founder, no less. "Sometimes father really does know best," the presentation slides quip.[12]

In teaching employees your brand culture, some may jokingly ask, "Will there be a test?" There is one at Altra Federal Credit Union. The LaCrosse, Wisconsin–based financial institution regularly uses surveys to get a feel for how well employees understand their values. They then share the results to keep everyone on the same page.

"A brand shouldn't be something you enforce. It should be something that inspires," says Jen Slaski. Around the Spiceworks office, she was commonly called the "Exec Brand Muse," as she was responsible for the essence of the Spiceworks brand. "Everything we do as employees translates into the brand."[13] Don't feel like the brand police. Like Slaski, you have to be your brand's muse, inspiring others to be a part of building your brand together.

"You have to build marketing inside-out today. It has to come from inside the company," says John Zissimos, Chief Creative Officer for cloud-computing giant Salesforce. "A brand is a promise. Usually in three dimensions. It's about the products, the people, and the vision of the future set by the CEO."[14] Your people have to understand this inside and out to realize their full potential as brand advocates.

The Forgotten Middle Circle

In thinking about people related to your brand, few make it past the general categories of employees and customers. When you consider all your vendors, strategic alliances, distribution channels, service providers, franchisees, affiliates, investors, bankers, sponsors, and everyone else that helps you do what you do, the list can get long.

In some cases, these individuals are even responsible for a key step in your customer's journey. That's certainly the case with IKEA. Their shipping partners deliver products to customers who live in states without an IKEA store. Like, say . . . Iowa, for example. As the old saying goes, you reap what you sow. If you treat these partners like outsiders—like vendors—they will act like vendors. If instead you treat these people as you treat your own—as trusted partners in delivering your brand experience—that's exactly what you'll get.

It's this philosophy that led the company to create the IKEA Way or I-Way. This credo is a broad list of values ranging from environmental commitments to employee working standards. At IKEA, the I-Way applies to everyone. From vendors to strategic alliances. Everyone is on the same page.

I struggle with which circle to put the Coldwell Banker realtors in. As licensees, they could technically be in this circle, too. It doesn't really matter. They understand the brand and know how to share the story. The Zappos Culture Book features an entire section with testimonials from partners such as Brooks, UGG Australia, and Oakley. "Zappos means 'YES, IT IS POSSIBLE!!!' Whether it is a deadline, fixing a problem, or taking care of a customer . . . every single time," says Sam G. of Saucony.[15]

Don't forget about this critical circle. Good brands engage their employees. Great brands with standout experiences know that the people involved with their brand consist of more than just those on their payroll.

Not All Outer Circles Are Equal

Making up the outer orbits of your brand's circles of community are your customers. As noted previously, these circles are of different sizes and varying importance.

You have to start with your best customers. Your loyal customers. Your raving fans. Are you treating them differently? Do you have a plan for how they can share with others the experiences they're having with your brand? This group may not be the biggest, but it is the pulse of your customer community. "Too many organizations care about numbers, not fans," says marketing legend Seth Godin. "What they're missing is the depth and interconnection that true fans deliver."

In some businesses, it's easy to keep your fans top-of-mind. As Executive Vice President & Chief Marketing Officer of the Minnesota Vikings, Steve LaCroix is responsible for everything from marketing and revenue generation to many aspects of the new stadium. "Don't lose sight of your fans," says LaCroix. "At the end of the day, we're in the entertainment business. We're looking at how to engage with our fans all year—even during the off-season."[16]

Focus on the people already in your business today. Your happy customers. Find new ways to embrace them online and off, and encourage them to share the experiences they're having with your brand. For my skating-rink owners and operators, this circle is represented by the customers skating today and enjoying themselves. How are you pleasing them? How are you creating unique brand experiences that they want to be a part of and, more importantly, share with their friends online? Can you hang a selfie frame in your rink? Can you gamify user-generated content by encouraging fan photos during limbo contests and snowball skates? If you're doing your job right, they're already having fun. You just need to encourage them to share in this.

In an effort to get to know their customers better, Spiceworks turned a road trip into ad-hoc fan research (or maybe it was vice versa). "In the beginning, the founders hit the road and talked to other IT professionals," says Jen Slaski. "Getting to know people drove everyone's work. These authentic, human relationships were at the heart of everything. We developed a deep respect for these people. It doesn't have to be a three-month focus group. Invite a few customers out for a beer."[17]

Try taking a road trip—even a short one—to get to know your best customers better. You can use this insight to enhance your brand experience for these special members of your community. Maybe you can even turn the spotlight on them. Each year, Salesforce takes over their hometown of San Francisco and invites hundreds of thousands of customers from throughout the globe to Dreamforce, the largest user-group event in the world. It's a must-attend for members of the Salesforce community.

In preparation for the event, the company promotes "The Road to Dreamforce," highlighting their best customers. When they heard that Garry Polmateer, founder of Red Argyle, a Salesforce-driven consulting company, had built a model of Dreamforce entirely out of LEGO bricks, they knew they had to do something. They created a video that came as close as one can to capturing Garry's energy as he provides a tour of his LEGO Dreamforce, while banging away at the drums.

Videos like Garry's are great for engaging the next circle out—the rest of your customers. Your best customers often have stories that you can use to engage the masses. They're already doing business with you. How can you excite them even more? LEGO comes into play again when you consider how it engages its very specific customer groups. For example, the company discovered that there was an abundance of adult LEGO fans. It put a plan in place to embrace and engage these AFOL (Adult Fans of LEGO) with online communities, events, and collaborations with LEGO executives. For the adult fans, collaborations have allowed them to influence the brand's business decisions, including developing new products like the LEGO Architecture series, featuring LEGO sets of iconic buildings such as the White House and Falling Water.

Maybe you can encourage your community members to create user-generated content like GoPro does. To help identify rabid fans and to transform average customers into the same, some brands develop structured brand ambassadorships. Maker's Mark has a brand-ambassador program that provides customers with special benefits, including their own barrel at the distillery and official ambassador business cards to share with friends. What sounds like a fun program accomplishes a very strategic objective in arming customers with tools to tell the brand's story.

As we make our way to the outer circles once again, the name says it all. This circle is called "almost out" for a reason. They're near the edge because they've been a customer in the most basic, transactional sense of the word. They've done business with you, but for whatever reason—maybe a bad experience, maybe they never felt special—they aren't in one of your inner circles. Put a plan in place for moving them back to the center. Once they bounce out to the outer circle, they'll be harder to bring back in (and more expensive).

After you cover your customer circles, you can start to focus on your prospects and potential customers in the outer circles. This outreach is where too many start. Don't make this mistake. Prospecting and lead generation are key, but not at the expense of caring for your best customers. Your inner circles.

Sounds simple, right? And yet too often we spend too much time focusing on the people who aren't anywhere near our businesses. Retailers exhaust themselves trying to appeal to new customers. Brands make comprehensive plans for dealing with upset customers without any kind of system for elevating passionate, happy fans. That's not to say that these groups aren't important. But when it comes to your limited time and resources, you need to spend more where you'll get more in return.

With so many marketing opportunities today—Facebook, Twitter, Instagram, LinkedIn, Snapchat, blogging, podcasting, and so on— you have to focus your work. To do so, you have to make sure you're focusing on the right people first.

Dynamic Circles and Brand Gravity

At the risk of overextending my space and science-fiction metaphors for this chapter, let me close by saying that beyond the concentric circles—the orbits of community that you need to follow—there's another dynamic at play. It's a dynamic that's a good example of brand-building in the digital age.

In the mass-media era, we were defined by marketing to the masses through broadcast advertising. Or outbound marketing.

Companies such as Hubspot have redefined our current era by popularizing inbound marketing. This is a shift in dynamics, as today we're drawing customers into our brands and onto our websites with our online content. Instead of the labels of inbound vs. outbound, I encourage you to think of this as creating brand gravity that pulls your community in.

This is accomplished through all the dynamics in this book with a special emphasis on the last three—story, content, and community. Story matters. It's the pattern of meaning that's easy to remember and easy to share. Content is the form that this sharing takes. And, finally, community is who does the sharing. American Express uses their Open Forum blog, a resource for the small business owners they serve, to create brand gravity.

Flow Hive creates gravity that inspires others as well. Adam Buchanan describes himself on his Twitter profile as a digital marketer, social media strategist, and beekeeper! Adam is a braver man than I. Motivated to become an amateur beekeeper by Flow Hive's innovative product and helpful content, Adam is now creating content on his website (adamcbuchanan.com) to share his adventures in beekeeping and help others along the way. Flow Hive inspires Adam, Adam inspires others, and so on and so forth.

Some call this "stickiness," but I like gravity better. Stickiness is a trap you lay. Gravity pulls people in over time and is irrefutable. To create brand gravity around your stories and content, you need to build your community. And to do that, you have to work your circles.

Everyone is responsible for brand activation. However, they can only do this with leadership from you. If this were the Starship *Enterprise*, you'd be in the captain's chair. In the words of Jean-Luc Picard, "Engage!"

BUILDING BLOCKS

- Think of the concentric circles outlined here. What would your circles look like?

- Draw the circles and sketch in who's sitting in each circle. What can you do for them? Is there content that you can create to help them meet their needs?

- Can you help those in your outer customer circles move toward the center—closer to being raving fans?

- How can you empower your brand ambassadors? Could you develop a structured program like Maker's Mark?

- What's a combination of story, content, and community that you can use to create brand gravity like American Express's Open Forum?

SIX
Clarity

So, this is where we are right now: Create a brand with meaning. A brand that stands for something. Structure it with touchpoints that build on your meaning and promise to your customers. Tell stories through engaging content that your employees, partners, customers, and other community members can help you create and share.

Some of the tools have changed, but these first few dynamics—in some form or another—have been around since the early caveman days. Back when the most innovative of cavemen would drag his knuckles out of his cave, proud of his amazing new club, which featured an ergonomic handle for a more comfortable prey-beating experience.

"My club is better than most and designed for hardworking cave people like you," he shared via a series of grunts. He scrawled out how well it worked on a cave wall and encouraged his cave-dwelling colleagues to look at his early content and hopefully buy his new product (in the form of trading him something else of value for it). If they liked it, they bought it and shared his brand (again, via grunt) with the rest of their community.

Or he used the aforementioned ergonomic club to beat them senseless until they bought.

Regardless, create a brand, tell a story, get attention. We've traded cave walls for paper and printing presses and eventually broadcast communication and the Internet. What's different today is something of a divergent challenge. On one hand, it's noisier than ever before. Remember what Eric Schmidt from Google said? The content on the Internet basically doubles itself every couple of days. And recall Schaefer's idea of "content shock"? We are all adding even more clutter to the marketplace. All this noise matters because, as brand-builders, we're trying to stand out.

The second issue can seem a bit contradictory. In spite of all the noise, the truth is more present than it's ever been. Traditionally, branding was simply grafting a message—customer-friendly or maybe just entertaining—onto an organization. In many cases, these stories weren't even based in reality.

A prime example is mid-century cigarette advertising. Tobacco companies panicked as people finally realized through science and *all the cancer* that perhaps the pack-a-day habit might not be the healthiest thing in the world. Their answer? Let's brand ourselves as a healthy alternative! These ads stressed that "more doctors smoke Camels than any other cigarette" and "viceroys filter the smoke—as your dentist recommends." Chesterfield boasted ten months of "scientific research."

It's easy to look back at this and laugh. But it's a cruel and evil use of a powerful art and science. For those in the profession of branding, this was a dark time. Sorry to depress you, but I can at least pick you back up pretty fast—this kind of public health crime isn't possible today, thanks to the Internet. People can do their own research, watchdog groups can fact-check corporate science, and all this can spread just as fast as misinformation. You can't hide from the truth today.

This creates a very different ecosystem for brands. But it's one that can be better navigated through an understanding of clarity. No, we're not buying diamonds. But in brand-building, clarity is helpful. There are a couple of ways to interpret clarity. The first definition in the dictionary tells us that it's a "clearness or lucidity as to perception or understanding." The second definition states that it's a "quality of being clear or transparent to the eye."[1]

Clarity is transparency and simplicity. Both are useful to the modern brand builder.

"If You Lie, You Die."

When I returned to my hotel after my pilgrimage to the first Starbucks on that rainy Seattle day, I sat down for a Skype chat with my friend Tamsen Webster. She's a master strategist, storyteller, and speaker. Her Red Thread video and event series (referenced in "Further Reading and Resources") encourages people to find the "red thread" or through line that ties everything together and creates meaning. When there's alignment, you have a powerful, clear brand that stands for something.

But what happens when there's a disconnect? Tamsen reminded me of one of the biggest examples of this—United Airlines. The message they've been branding *at* us is to "Fly the Friendly Skies."[2] That's what they promise. What they deliver is anything but friendly.

Since I started teaching Social Media Marketing at the University of Iowa, I've referenced Dave Carroll's oft-told story about United breaking his guitar. The short recap: In 2009, Carroll was in a band called Sons of Maxwell. As they flew United for a gig, he observed the baggage handlers throwing his Taylor guitar, ultimately breaking it. He sought reparations from United, who chose not to respond.

Carroll, in turn, created the song and accompanying music video "United Breaks Guitars" documenting his sad tale. The now-famous viral video has garnered more than 17 million views on YouTube and is featured as a social customer-service case study in countless marketing classes and books.[3] The punch line? Carroll now has a profitable career as a professional speaker. His topic? Customer service.

I've told this story so many times through the years that I actually started wondering while talking to Tamsen on that rainy Seattle day: Will United ever be forgiven for this epic brand failure? Is it time to let them out of the doghouse? Fate answered my question the following week.

That's when United had passenger David Dao violently dragged off of an overbooked flight, resulting in a concussion and broken nose. With a hit to their stock, rounds of tone-deaf corporate responses, and boycotts from social media users globally, they should probably stay in the doghouse for a while. What the rest of us can learn from this is the importance of transparency.

Trust is in short supply today. Each year since 2001, PR giant Edelman publishes the results of their annual Trust Barometer. Trust in institutions of all kinds—from governments and NGOs to businesses and media—is down.[4] Nielsen shows that only 33 percent of online consumers trust advertising.[5]

"Today, if you lie, you die," says David B. Srere, co-CEO and chief strategy officer of global brand strategy, design, and experience firm Siegel+Gale. In the past, an upset customer would tell twenty people and maybe a few would stop going to your business as a result. Now those upset customers are telling the world through social media. Watch the video of David Dao being dragged off the United flight, and you'll see passengers aghast *and* taking photos and video with their phones. "There's got to be a connection between what a brand promises and what they do. People want authenticity and today they can check you on it," cautions Srere.[6]

What can your brand do to build trust? Be transparent in what you say and what you do. The Edelman Trust Barometer notes that 55 percent of the general population says that businesses can build trust by being more transparent.[7] A study from Label Insight reports that 94 percent of all consumers are more likely to be loyal to a brand when it commits to full transparency.[8] Furthermore, 81 percent said they would be willing to sample a brand's entire range of products if they were comfortable with the brand's transparency.[9]

You can't advertise your way to a better, stronger brand today. First, as the data shows, most of the public doesn't even believe your ads. "Brands can't bullshit anymore," says Porter Gale, start-up adviser and former vice president of marketing at Virgin America. "There's too much information out there."[10] Instead of clever ads, focus on building a clear, transparent brand with no daylight between what you say and what you do.

It's harder work, for sure. But, as former Patagonia Director of Environmental Strategy Jill Dumain quips, "Clarity is the new clever."[11]

And Patagonia would know.

With Transparency, You Get What You Give

More than a 1998 one-hit wonder from the New Radicals, "you get what you give" could also serve as a pretty decent brand ethos. Transparency in your business practices—what you say, what you do, where your products come from—is key to building a standout brand.

In the outdoor-clothing space, Patagonia stands out. But they do so in a very nontraditional way. As previously cited, they'd prefer you not buy more jackets unless you really need them. They stand for something bigger. As the company's mission states, they strive to "build the best product, cause no unnecessary harm, use business to inspire and implement solutions to the environmental crisis."[12]

That's fine to say. Many companies may say something similar. But to stand out today, you have to actually walk that talk. Committed to sustainable environmental practices and minimizing their footprint, Patagonia recently launched a new initiative taking this approach even further. Used merchandise can now be returned for new merchandise credits. The used clothing is then cleaned and repaired and sold on their "Worn Wear" website.

Patagonia founder Yvon Chouinard commits 1 percent of their total sales or 10 percent of their profit, whichever is more, to environmental groups. He went on to found One Percent for the Planet, an organization that encourages other businesses to do the same. "Every time I made the decision because it was the right thing to do, I've ended up making more money," says Chouinard.[13]

A cynic might write this off as simply giving back. But it's bigger than that. Plus, "giving back implies that you've taken something away," as Denise Lee Yohn writes in *What Great Brands Do*.[14] Environmental impact and sustainability provide big opportunities for brand transparency. However, you can also see transparency in a business's core beliefs and smaller day-to-day acts.

The word *chobani* comes from the Persian word *çoban*, meaning "shepherd."[15] But to most, Chobani is synonymous with the top-selling Greek yogurt in the United States. Probably the most obsessive, Steve Jobs–like thing in my repertoire is religiously starting every day with a cup of Cho to go with my cup of joe. I'm not alone.

Transparency has been key to the growth of this dominant Greek yogurt brand. As their name derivation suggests, shepherds guide and teach. The core belief at Chobani, as stated on their website, is a simple one: they want to provide better food to more people.[16] That's why Chobani is committed to all-natural, non-GMO ingredients. They communicate this clearly and with great transparency.

However, a big hang-up in striking a balance between food quality and quantity is food safety. In 2013, when a common mold species was found in their yogurt, Chobani announced a broad voluntary recall. Moreover, they stopped all marketing promotion, and founder, CEO, and Chairman Hamdi Ulukay took over their social networks to reassure customers. This also provided an opportunity for the shepherd to educate the public on the mold found, *Mucor circinelloides*, as opposed to the sensationalizing that often happens in the media.

An attack on a core belief could have sunk a lesser brand. The answer once again is found in transparency. In the case of Chobani, this response is logical because of the connection to who they are and what they stand for. Transparency makes it easier for your message to be effectively sent and received. That's how transparency contributes to clarity.

Another strategy for getting your brand to stand out? Don't overcomplicate it in the first place.

Swedish Simplicity

In the middle of writing this book, our family moved. If you're wondering about the writer's routine and such, I would not recommend this. Like any move, some of our furniture fit in our new house, and we moved it in. Other stuff didn't, and we got rid of it. And there were a few pieces we needed that we ordered new.

One was a printer stand for my home office. I ordered something pretty basic from Amazon. We also needed a new bookcase for our swollen collection of books. We had some fun here and ordered a big shelf with glass doors from IKEA. The printer stand came. I unpacked the usual fare—boards, screws, casters, and the like. All were labeled not once, but twice. G1 is also "cabinet shelf," B2-Left is "drawer one left," and so forth. It was a bit tricky to follow. Somewhere on the package, it suggested a 30-minute assembly time. I finished in just over an hour.

Ironically, our massive IKEA shelf arrived on the same day. As Iowans, we are IKEA-less. We've stopped in before while on trips elsewhere, but the brand is not a routine part of our lives. So this was my first experience assembling my very own Swedish master-piece. After studying Ariely's IKEA Effect mentioned in Chapter One, I was ready to work hard for my shelf. If I suffered, I would be rewarded with meaning.

First, I was stunned to discover upon unloading the box that the parts weren't labeled. How would I know what all these pieces were?! *To the manual!* As I flipped through the instructions, I couldn't find any words explaining what I was supposed to do! There were just . . . easy-to-follow diagrams with circles calling out key points with close-up images of assembly. I took a deep breath and followed along. And that's when something crazy happened.

It just worked. It came together seamlessly, with minimal sweat and profanity. I had trouble not shouting out, like Tom Hanks in *Cast Away*, "Look what I have created!!!" (If I'm being honest, I'm prone to shouting this after most pedestrian activities such as making tacos on a weeknight.)

The meaning achieved through the IKEA Effect is not one built on toiling and excruciating labor: rather, it's one of simplicity. IKEA is simple in every way imaginable. From big products like my shelf to smaller kitchen utensils to their cavernous in-store experience featuring the aforementioned flat boxes ready for assembly (and meaning; not to mention the fact that this brand spark is also cheaper to store and ship). All is designed using Spartan Scandinavian minimalism featuring simple visual instructions.

But IKEA isn't just a brand that embraces simplicity. They embrace both aspects of clarity. In the previous chapter, we looked at their transparency on a range of values from employee working standards to the environment, both internally among their employees and externally with their partners and vendors.

In a world as noisy and cluttered as ours, packed full of content and marketing messages that never make it to their intended audience, attention spans are shrinking. A message of simplicity should be an easy sell. And yet all we can do is keep creating. More content. More posts. More videos. More live video. More social networks. More stories. More stories on more social networks.

Why is simplicity so hard?

Get More by Doing Less

As I type this section heading, I feel gross. Not gross. I feel like a stereotypical ad man. Cast in the worst light, a con man. Getting more by doing less?!? That's insane. I might as well be promising high quality and low prices. It's unbelievable, but it's true. You can get more attention—at one of the hardest times for doing so—by doing less of what everyone else is doing and more of what only you can do. Focus is the key to simplicity.

In building brands, it's easy to get caught in the trap that making something better is an additive process. To build a better brand, we have to make it more complex. Add messages and logos. Bloated brand families with logos and sub-logos. Mission statements, taglines, and campaign slogans. I shudder as organizations stress "How easy we've made it to use our brand assets," followed by a step-by-step walk through a complex system that's anything but easy. Hint: If you have trouble making sense of your brand internally, it's time to simplify.

Start by subtracting. If your brand's meaning is defined—your spark and promise—use that as a tool for pruning your overgrown brand. One of the more common examples in brand simplicity played out in the great search-engine wars. But first, let me set this up with an aside about Midwesterners.

A common misconception about Iowans and others from the Midwest is that we're nice. That we're not snobs. Well, we're not

always nice. And we can be snobs. We're just quiet about it. For example, when standing over someone's shoulder while they open up
a browser to show me something, I stand in quiet, snobby judgment
if your browser is set to Yahoo's home page. Or, really, anything
that's not Google. That's because, as they've proven time and again,
no one is better at search than Google. In fact, their mission is "to
organize the world's information and make it universally accessible
and useful."

Their mission is at work everywhere. Especially on the Google
home page. That stark white page with their logo (or a topical
"doodle" based on a holiday or historic observation) and a big open
search box. It's always been like this. For contrast, look at Yahoo.
Sure, they've introduced a Google-like experience with a simplified logo and more white space, but the search bar is surrounded
by other features. News, trending topics, online display ads—both
fixed and retargeting ads. I don't want any of this. I want to search!
That's why Google commands an overwhelming share of mobile
and desktop searches, both in the United States and globally.

Subtracting and simplifying has helped the Google brand stand
out. That's because subtracting and simplifying helps *meaning* stand
out. What can you subtract from your experience to amplify your
meaning?

Simple is literally in the Simplisafe name. The start-up, founded
by husband and wife Chad and Eleanor Laurans, found an innovative way to capitalize on the challenges of the home security
industry. Specifically—home security is complicated. While most
value home security, the market is defined by big players and ag-
gressive sales teams looking to sell you as many devices as possible.

This all adds up to a high overall cost. You can order Simplisafe devices online and install them yourself. And there's no lengthy contract. You pay $15 a month. Or you don't. You're safe and secure. It's that simple.

Simplicity and transparency often go hand in hand. Our fast digital world has other implications beyond brands and content. We're also busier than ever before. That means convenient, nutrient-packed meals are more important than ever. Hard-core coders in Silicon Valley have taken this trend literally with their affinity for the aptly named Soylet, a sludge shake you can eat at your desk, *so you never have to stop coding.* Eating on the go doesn't have to be so . . . extreme.

Rxbars is a Chicago-based start-up that aims to provide a simple meal-replacement experience for those not interested in re-creating a dystopian Charlton Heston sci-fi classic ("*Soylent Green* is people!!"). The brand is built on their minimalist approach to protein bars, which contain only a handful of ingredients. This simplicity is communicated with transparency. Their packaging is simply a list of ingredients. As a Maple Sea Salt bar notes: 3 egg whites, 5 pecans, 4 cashews, 2 dates, no BS. The final ingredient gets them extra points for brand voice. And by BS, they mean no added sugar, dairy, soy, gluten, GMOs, or preservatives. Many have noted that the bars may not win a taste test against popular options like Kind Plus bars; but Rxbars offer three times as much protein. Focus. Simplicity. Transparency. A winning recipe.

These popular examples demonstrate the power of simplicity. In a crowded, cluttered marketplace, brands that are able to reduce the noise and provide pleasing communications and experiences will earn a special place in the hearts and minds of customers. More isn't always better. Sometimes more is just more.

Clarity Accelerates Movement

We struggle with branding for many of the same reasons we struggle with simplicity. As humans, we intrinsically think that accomplishment follows complexity. Something that's more advanced is better because it has more pieces. It feels right. Simplicity is scary. Shouldn't we hedge our bet that more people will like us by adding more features? More messages? More ways someone can use our product or service?

Likewise, the best brand-building advice is easy to miss because it doesn't feel right. *Stand for something? Tell stories? Create content and community? Be honest, open, and transparent?* Okay. But what's the real secret? All that stuff is nice but that can't be it. It's too . . . simple.

But simple matters. More importantly, simple pays. Each year, global brand strategy firm Siegel+Gale releases the findings of their Global Brand Simplicity Index™ (www.simplicityindex.com). Recent research shows that 64 percent of consumers are willing to pay more for simpler experiences, and 61 percent of consumers are more likely to recommend a brand because it's simple.[17] Simplicity is winning. And the market is in need of clarity. While Edison Research reports that a third of Americans knowingly follow brands on social media, few understand what any of them are saying.[18] In his groundbreaking documentary on the age of brand transparency, *The Naked Brand*, Jeffrey Rosenbaum cites a 21 percent drop in people who say they understand brands.[19]

So how can you find clarity? Jay Acunzo, host of the *Unthinkable* podcast and former Google employee, recommends the simple practice of "why-ing something to death." How does this work? It's simple. (See what I did there?) The next time you're doing some-thing—adding a product extension, launching a new marketing campaign—ask yourself *why* you're doing this. And then, ask *why* again about the answer given. Once you have that answer, ask *why* again. And again. How long does it take you to get close to your brand's meaning? To your spark and promise? This is how you keep your brand focused, simple, and clear.

Think back to the famous Google search home page. Don't you think that there were people during the company's history who championed adding things to this high-traffic online destination? But Google said no. A series of *whys* would very quickly lead back to their mission of organizing information. Clutter gets in the way of this. "If you 'why' something to death, you'll find clarity," says Acunzo.[20]

Another key to clarity? A fresh set of eyes. Someone who can see what you can't. "Sometimes you need someone from outside your fish bowl to deliver the clarity of simple insights," says David Srere of Siegel+Gale, a branding firm so built on simplicity that they famously helped the IRS create the 1040EZ simplified tax form.[21]

When your brand is transparent and simple, it's easier to un-derstand. It's easier for your audience to gain meaning. That's why transparent, simple brands move faster than the opaque, complex alternatives.

BUILDING BLOCKS

- How transparent is your brand? Are there any gaps between what you say and what you do?

- Are there elements of your brand—who you are, what you say, etc.—that you can subtract to amplify your meaning and stand out?

- What can you "why to death" when it comes to your brand?

- Here are some idea starters for places you can simplify your brand:
    - *Brand name:* think Simplisafe (more on naming in the Brand Now Toolbox)
    - *Brand promise:* don't over-slogan your brand
    - *Products and services:* don't overextend
    - *Brand names for your products and services:* don't over-brand
    - *Website navigation:* seriously, look at your navigation
    - *Content strategy:* don't produce more than you have to; avoid "me-too" content that looks and sounds just like everyone else

- Who can you ask from "outside of your fish bowl" to help you gain clarity?

SEVEN
Experience

With five kids, vacations by car are an economic necessity. If you get past the constant bickering, the endless stretches of barren highway (thank you, Nebraska), and the intricacies of planning bathroom logistics for five small humans—some of whom don't completely understand bladder control—it's actually quite relaxing. As someone who's crisscrossed our nation's highways and byways, there's also no shortages of attractions on roadside billboards beckoning you to stop. Like the signs for the SPAM Museum we constantly pass on I-35 outside Austin, Minnesota. "See famous porks of art," the billboards promise.

Returning from a recent family trip to the Twin Cities, I shared a knowing look with my wife that said: "We aren't on a tight schedule. We've got nowhere to be—the world is our oyster. It's time for the SPAM Museum." On our way into Austin, we discover that this is the *new* location for the SPAM Museum. Yes, the SPAM Museum has been so successful, they've expanded into newer and more elaborate digs situated in the center of downtown (or "uptown," as one might be inclined to say here).

The first "pork of art" you see on approach is just that: a majestic statue of a farmer walking alongside two pigs greeting you at the museum's entrance. As you step through the front doors, a massive interactive exhibit draws you in. It looks like the New York Stock Exchange. Huge SPAM logos and giant screens showcasing videos of SPAM in the news, SPAM fan stories, and the like. A wheel spins with fun facts about the product under the headline "There's a lot to learn about the SPAM brand" (for example, "There are 12.8 cans of SPAM eaten every second").[1]

As you venture deeper, you discover exhibits on how the curious product is made (just six ingredients), complete with an assembly line for kids featuring their iconic square cans. Another hall takes you through the history of SPAM including a stop at a re-creation of a World War II army camp featuring a full-size Jeep as panels teach you about the role of SPAM in the war effort (SPAM offered a solution to the challenges of getting meat to the front lines). Still another hall takes you through "SPAM in the World" with exhibits on how SPAM is used in countries such as the United Kingdom (home of the SPAMish Omelette) and South Korea (where SPAM outranks Coca-Cola in status).

This is about as concise a summary as I can offer while still doing justice to this roadside attraction. Needless to say, I was blown away. I left with a T-shirt and a coffee mug. And, yes, a can of SPAM. I also left with an insight that leads us to our seventh and final Brand Now dynamic.

SPAM is a pretty basic canned food. It is iconic partially because of how unremarkable it is. And yet parent company Hormel has built a powerful brand culture that comes to life and is celebrated throughout the world. That's because SPAM offers a vivid brand experience.

Which begs the question: If SPAM can do it, why can't you?

The Experience Problem

Each dynamic leading up to this point is critical. But everything—creating a brand with meaning, making promises, telling stories, sharing content, building community, getting clarity with transparency and simplicity—is nothing without experience. It's not enough to tell a story or make a promise. You have to *live* the story. And you do that by creating your experience.

What's tricky is that "experience" is not a finite item you can easily check off of your list. It's a lot of little things. "Branding is thousands of tiny punches that add up," says Stacie Grissom, Head of Content for BarkBox, the monthly subscription service of BARK.[2]

It could be easy to write off BarkBox as a simple online box service. But BARK makes a promise to dog parents that they live vividly both online and off. The experience doesn't start and stop with the box that gets shipped to your door. It begins with engaging online content with stories such as "15 Dachshunds Who Need Their Ears Reset," and it continues with live events such as their "Open Bark Nights" and BarkFest in Brooklyn.

Simply put, experience is your brand promise delivered. Remember how John Michael Morgan, author of *Brand Against the*

Machine, said that what we're actually selling is the in-between? That in-between is made up of thousands of tiny punches and can be hard to tackle. But brand-builders can't afford to skip this challenging, yet critical, dynamic.

In your gut, you probably have a hunch that tells you that the best customer experience wins. But there's actually data that backs this up. Customer experience firm Watermark Consulting conducted a groundbreaking six-year analysis of stock market returns for companies that lead in customer experience versus those that lag.

"Customer experience leaders outperformed the broader market, generating a total return that was three times higher on average than the S&P 500," details Watermark founder Jon Picoult.[3] Furthermore, 80 percent of customers say they would stop using a brand after just one bad brand experience, according to a study from LogMeIn. And 72 percent of them would advise family and friends to stop, too![4] This is all the result of one bad experience.

"Many business leaders pay lip service to customer-experience excellence, reflecting a deep-seated skepticism about the value of such differentiation," continues Picoult. "The benefits are often viewed as soft and difficult to quantify, so companies continue to subject consumers to complicated sales processes, cluttered websites, dizzying 800-line menus, long wait times, incompetent customer service, unintelligible correspondence, and products that are just plain difficult to use."[5]

Lip service sounds about right. The Chartered Institute of Marketing found that 70 percent of marketers believe investing in experience is effective. But only 13 percent believe their brand excels at delivering it.[6]

When you add all this up, it's clear that experience can deliver long-term value, while bad experiences—even one—are barriers to loyalty. Most agree experience is critical, but few deliver on it. And that's a gap we need to address. "We woke up and all of a sudden we weren't in the marketing business anymore," says Siegel+Gale's David B. Srere. "We're in the experience business now."[7]

How can you create a better brand experience?

Mapping a Better Brand Experience

When asked how to take on the challenge of brand experience, I'm reminded of a scene from the 1962 movie *To Kill a Mockingbird*, based on Harper Lee's classic book. Gregory Peck as Atticus Finch is sitting in a creaky porch swing with his arm around his young daughter, Scout. She's struggled with her first day of school. Pushing his glasses back up onto the bridge of his nose, Atticus says she's learned a valuable lesson. He tells her that you can't understand a person until you see things from that person's perspective. "Until you climb into his skin and walk around in it."[8]

You can use this valuable lesson in your work as a brand-builder as well. To craft a memorable brand experience, you have to start considering things from your customer's point of view. In the digital age, you can get quite literal with this advice. Justine Jordan is the Vice President of Marketing at Litmus. Responsible for brand experience at the email marketing software provider, she often takes Atticus's words to heart. That's why, every few months, Justine clears her browser's cache and spends time rediscovering the Litmus brand online.

"Despite having worked here for five years and having used the software for eight years, I regularly go back and sign up for our emails or go through our new-user onboarding experience," says Jordan. "You have to put yourself in the shoes of the user and say 'Does this make sense?' Walk through how a user interacts with your brand. That's designing an experience. It requires critical thinking and empathy. So many marketers have never walked a mile in their user's shoes." You should conduct brand-experience audits across channels regularly. "Do this every quarter or every six months," advises Jordan.[9]

To help organize both your audit and your brand experience, consider creating a touchpoint map. Lest you think we're making an already complex topic—brand experience—even more complex by introducing mapmaking, fear not. There's no advanced cartography required in mapping your brand experience. You just need to draw one shape a few different times. And it's probably one of the first shapes you drew as a child.

In addition to helping you organize your brand's community, concentric circles can also help you audit your brand experience. Start with the center circle. This is your Core Brand DNA—your spark, name, logo, brand promise, and core story. It's the first few dynamics we discussed. As the DNA metaphor suggests, these pieces inform the rest of your brand touchpoints.

Your next circle out is not your marketing. Not yet. With community, the danger is in leaping all the way to the outer circles of transactional customers and prospects. With brand experience, it's easy to focus only on marketing touchpoints. When you do this, you miss other experiential opportunities along the way. Your next circle should be your Product/Service Experience. Use this circle to map out your various products and services, both what they are and where your customers can find them. Do they come to your store? Do they go to your website? How can they buy what you sell? Are there order forms? Service staff they interact with? Are there emails they receive? An onboarding process they go through? Is your packaging special? Everything directly related to your products and services goes in this circle.

The next circle out is your marketing communications. However, as marketing communications is complex, let's organize this circle a little bit. Draw two radial lines from the center of the circle out on each side. Label the top half of this circle "Static-Analog Touchpoints." Your television, radio, and print advertising, along with your direct mail, goes here. Label the bottom half "Interactive-Digital Touchpoints." Your website, email marketing, search, social media, and content marketing goes here.

Just for fun, add an outer circle called "Bonus." You can add any extra touchpoints here. Maybe your brand has a unique smell, like Aveda. Smell is no laughing matter. Nike showed that adding scents to their stores increased intent to purchase by 80 percent.[10] Or maybe you have signature lighting such as Virgin's in-flight mood lighting.

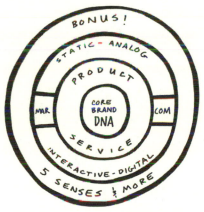

If you're not confident in your artistic skills, check out the Brand Now Toolbox for a touchpoint map you can fill out.

Now start filling in your touchpoint map. Leave no step of your experience uncharted. Think of Atticus and Justine and follow your customer. Make note of everything. What are your employees wearing? Is it a Hawaiian shirt like the Trader Joe's team? What does it say? How about your shipping boxes? If you're sending fashionable apparel, make sure your packaging continues that brand promise like Stitch Fix does. Each intricate package of curated clothing comes with personalized cards from your stylist. And don't forget your receipts. "There's a way to make receipts more interesting that doesn't also annoy everyone involved," says futurist comedian, writer, and cultural critic Baratunde Thurston. "A receipt can simply be a record of a transaction. But a receipt can also be a platform for creativity to extend the relationship between customers and merchants into something more interesting."[11]

For more advanced experience analysis, consider mapping your competitor's experience and then comparing it with yours. Are there things they're doing that you should be? Are there things neither of you is doing that present an opportunity for standing out? I'm not sure the marketplace was crying out for a mobile e-commerce experience that had a cat with laser eyes scan your credit card for payment, but that didn't stop Zappos. From parachuting products into your cart to seasonal decor, their mobile app is fun to use.

As you can see, getting your arms around your brand experience is no small task. It can also push you into obsessive-compulsive territory. As Denise Lee Yohn, author of *What Great Brands Do*, writes, "Great brands need to think big, but they try not to let those big thoughts distract them from sweating the small stuff."[12]

Ready to have your mind blown? Your map is 3-D—no special glasses required. Use your mind and take a look at the touchpoint map. The center Core Brand circle is the bottom—the deepest point.

Now the Product/Service layer—a little wider and a few levels up—followed by the wider-still Marketing-Communications layer. It's a funnel! You should be able to follow your customer through this experience funnel from the first ad they see on Facebook through the rest of your experience, until they are a core part of your brand.

With your touchpoints mapped, now what? We impose the mighty fist of branding on all of them, right? Wrong.

Consistency vs. Coherence

Hello. My name is Nick, and I've been called "The Brand Police" by my coworkers. As brand builders, we're an easy target with our standards and style guides. Sometimes the cool kids rebel and run their own ads. To be fair, we are a little fixed on consistency. Once we map out a brand experience, it's easy to continue down that path by standardizing everything. *Make it all the same! All of it!*

But branding has changed. Where we were formerly focused on consistency, today's digital dynamics call for more flexible systems. Instead of focusing on making all our brand touchpoints consistent, we need to focus on coherence. When something is coherent, it's *logically or aesthetically ordered or integrated* or *having the quality of holding together or cohering.*[13]

"Some are very rigid and want everything to look exactly alike across products and channels and some are much looser," says Barbara Apple Sullivan, managing partner at brand consultancy Sullivan. "It's more about coherence and what the brand stands for than consistency. To be effective and evolve and be relevant in the various channels, it's about training people to understand the true value and meaning of that brand so that as they're creating it in the specific environments, it can be coherent and stand for and mean the same thing. It always ladders up through that customer experience."[14]

Consider Google again. While most brand standards start with what you can and can't do with the logo, Google bends what their logo is almost every day. Their Google Doodles are the fun, surprising, and sometimes spontaneous changes made to the Google logo to celebrate holidays, anniversaries, and the lives of famous artists, pioneers, and scientists. From Mary Pickford's birthday to the 105th anniversary of the first expedition to the North Pole, Google changes their logo—a critical element on the aforementioned simple home page—constantly. They even encourage the public to submit ideas. That's not how branding is supposed to work!

"Great brands demonstrate unity, not uniformity," says Josh Miles, principal of Indianapolis-based branding firm Miles Herndon and author of the book *Bold Brand 2.0.* "Uniformity means if you lay it all out, it all looks the same. Everything is just a clone. Unity means there are plenty of things that tie it together. When you see a Target ad, you know what it is before the bullseye logo appears at the end. There are things visually with tone. As brand builders, we have to know what those most important touchpoints are."[15]

As you look at every tiny piece of your brand experience, it's that much more important to understand what your brand stands for. That way, you can infuse the touchpoint with the perfect amount of meaning for where the customer is at this point in your experience. What works on Facebook may not work on your showroom floor. Frameworks such as font, color, personality, and tone will contextualize what you're saying and make it clear that it's from your brand, as Miles notes; but to stand out, you have to explore the freedom to say different things in different places.[16]

Bathroom spray Poo~Pourri has a unique brand experience that they build with coherent touchpoints. Looking at the Product/Service circle, their packaging discards the garish aerosols that the rest of the bathroom-spray category embraces. Their bottle looks more like a perfume or lotion. "I hated those ugly cans. Plus I loved the juxtaposition of beauty and toilet spray," says Suzy Batiz, founder and CEO of Poo~Pourri.[17] Their distinct brand voice adds to that juxtaposition with spray names like "Trap a Crap" (cedarwood + citrus) and "Potty Potion" (rosemary + tea tree + lavender).

When it came time to tell their story with video, instead of literally bringing their unique bottles to life anthropomorphically as others might, they personified this beauty literally—with a prim and proper redheaded British woman. However, she continues the voice and the juxtaposition as she says, while sitting on a toilet in a party dress, "You would not believe the motherlode I just dropped. . . . While flushing removes the physical evidence . . . what can be done of that subtle scent of a 300-cow dairy farm? How do you make the world believe your poop doesn't stink? Poo~Pourri is the before-you-go toilet spray that is proven to trap those embarrassing odors at the source . . . and save your relationships."[18] More than just being consistent across touchpoints, Poo~Pourri is coherent in their voice and the juxtaposition of their story.

This flexibility within frameworks allows you to empower both your internal and external brand advocates. "By building both autonomy and consistency, brands are better able to respond in real-time and at a local level," says Marc Shillum, Founder of Chief Creative Office.[19] What we need is consistency in our big big ideas and coherence within our executions, across our brand touchpoints. As Marty Neumeier writes in his book *The Brand Flip*, "Think of brand experiences as fractals of the overall brand."[20]

Don't get stuck being the brand police. Work with your team to build a culture that not only understands your brand; make sure they're empowered to create coherent experiences within their personal areas of the business. Speaking of which . . .

Let's Talk Culture

While we've talked about community, strong cultures help build strong brands. You can't have one without the other. This starts with your new employees—who you hire. That's why Suzy Batiz is still the last interview for all new hires at Poo~Pourri. That's also why BARK, the company behind BarkBox and BarkShop, only hires people who understand pets. "We only hire people who get dogs. Not everyone here has a dog, but we all value dogs," says BARK's Stacie Grissom.[21] You need that shared understanding right out of the gate.

At Maker's Mark, this happens on day one with the "big dose of history and culture" new employees receive through the brand presentation based on the founder's insights.[22] Brand history and culture is reinforced in similar ways at Coldwell Banker through their storybook and at Poo~Pourri. "We make the voice of our brand loud and pass stories like our ancestors did—by the campfire," says Batiz. "We have weekly lunch-and-learns or 'campfires' where we tell stories about the brand."[23]

It's also effective to leave your people with a touchstone or two to help them live your brand's values. Buffer is a social media management software company that exemplifies the kind of clarity discussed in the last chapter. If there's an issue with the product, you hear about it from them up front. For example, when they were hacked, they immediately published a post that was clearly titled "Here's what you need to know."[24] This kind of transparency requires a strong culture. To reinforce what they teach about the brand, everyone gets a sticker with the company values on it:

→ Choose positivity
→ Default to transparency
→ Focus on self-improvement
→ Be a no-ego doer
→ Listen first, then listen more
→ Communicate with clarity
→ Make time to reflect
→ Live smarter, not harder
→ Show gratitude
→ Do the right thing

Too often, organizations are too consumed with HR and other employee guidelines and policies to consider adding these doses of branding and culture. And yet few things can be so effective in helping your brand grow, especially when you consider creating a coherent brand experience across all touchpoints. In many cases, these touchpoints are managed and delivered by disparate parties internally. Maintaining a strong brand culture unifies your team and strengthens your brand at the same time. With a simple credo like what Buffer employees receive, you have what you need to be part of the brand experience at any level—from writing an email to answering customer questions.

To foster this organization-wide understanding of your brand, you should consider implementing a brand task force, as branding and marketing expert Drew McLellan advises. Who should be on this task force? "No more than twelve people. You should have worker bees—they see the company differently. You should also have those bigger thinkers who aren't territorial."[25] In addition to serving as your compass, task force members can also be cheerleaders helping you get buy-in on difficult decisions that are necessary to build a strong brand.

"Your people are your brand," says Thom Wyatt, Managing Director at Siegel+Gale. "Brands and corporate culture are inextricably linked. The strongest brands are emotionally engaging to both their customers and their employees."[26]

What are you doing to take those key pieces of your brand DNA, your meaning, what you stand for, your story, even your history, to those who need it most—your people?

The Divining Rod and the Planted Flag

Well . . . this is an awkward thing to confess at this late stage, but I don't know exactly *who* you are.

People who care about brands and branding come from varied backgrounds. Traditionally, branding people were agency types. However, as the discipline has grown and evolved, so too have those who make brand-building their business. I'm sure many of you are entrepreneurs who have started a business and built your brand from scratch. Others may work for those same visionary business leaders on marketing teams (or a team of one) at businesses big and small. You're trying to distill their dreams into brands and experiences that the world can interact with. And I know that many of you lead nonprofit organizations, government agencies, and other entities that are charged with building a brand that people want to connect with and be a part of—either through donations or advocacy. Or you may just be a personal brand, pursuing your own interests.

The truth is, it doesn't matter who you are. That sounded more callous than intended, but it doesn't matter, because brand-building is bigger than any one job description, department, or area on the organizational chart. As this exploration of brand experience has shown, branding is everything. This can be overwhelming, which is why brand-building should be everyone's business. But they can only help you if they know what to do.

Once your people know your brand—who you are and what you stand for—you can realize the even bigger power that comes from building a brand. Your brand has the potential to be more than just a marketing communications tool. Your brand is a divining rod that you can use to navigate your organization's growth. "It's a filter to make big decisions," says Drew McLellan.[27]

That's why CVS had to stop selling cigarettes: it didn't square with who they needed to be as a brand. It's why Tylenol famously told people not to buy their product, as some had been laced with cyanide. They didn't know the extent of the issue, but they knew who they were as a brand. It's why Patagonia wants you to buy their products, but not more than you need. And it's why Maker's Mark reversed their business decision to reduce the alcohol proof in their bourbon. Your brand isn't just your logo, ads, and packaging. It's what you stand for. When everyone understands this, you can march forward together in service of the same goals.

"A brand is aspirational," continues McLellan. "Think of it as a flag planted in the ground a ways off. You're always trying to get to it. You may not make it, but you strive to get as close to it as possible, as often as possible. Today when your brand breaks its promise, it's not met with a whisper. It's met with a shout."[28]

You may stumble, so make sure you have a plan for how to make it up to your customer when you break your brand promise.

Disney works to create an immaculate amusement park and resort experience. They knew people would litter, so they have trash cans located every 10 feet and all employees, called cast members, pick up the trash. When a guest's room isn't ready (a rarity), they respond with customized chocolate and VIP status. No one wants to fall short of the flag planted for your brand, but you will. Be ready. Have a plan in place.

While everyone is responsible for brand-building, your role is unique. You're like the producer of the movie. Responsible for the big idea that guides the entire show, along with coordinating the little pieces that inform everything else that you're not directly responsible for. It can be daunting, to be sure, but you're not alone.

After spending this much time with me, you probably realize that I love thinking about brands and working through the challenges they face. That's why I want to remind you to please email me about your brand. What are you struggling with? What have you done that inspired the rest of your team? What brands make you smile? My email address is nick@westergaard.com. I'm a branding nut and an email addict. I want to talk to you. We brand-builders are strange unicorns who think a bit differently than most. We have to stick together.

Remember, although technology has changed many things—how we get our information and how much we get—people are still searching harder than ever for meaning. They want to hear compelling stories. Standout brands deliver both, through structured touchpoints. If you build a brand that stands for something, people will want to be a part of it. They'll consume your content and join your community. But they'll expect clarity and a seamless experience that delivers on every aspect of your brand promise.

That's how you brand now.

And we're not even done. Not by a long shot. What follows in Part Two—The Brand Now Toolbox—is a set of tools in the form of tactical essays and frameworks on how to implement these dynamics in the service of particular types of brands (small-business, B2B, personal, political) or in specific situations (naming, crisis, experience). There's even a bonus dynamic (humor!). The following section is how you take the ideas of this book and put them to work for you.

You might keep reading straight through, or you may hop around based on who you are and what challenges you face. It's entirely up to you. It's your brand. Let's get started building it.

BUILDING BLOCKS

- Complete the touchpoint map using the three concentric circles described here. (There's a handy blank diagram for you in the toolbox ahead.) Once you're done, what are your three most important touchpoints? How could you do more with these moments in your customer experience?

- Remember my trip to the SPAM Museum? Is there some amazing, unexpected immersive experience you could offer your fans to celebrate their love of your brand?

- How can you make your brand—who you are and what you stand for—a part of your company's culture? Is there something you can do when you onboard new employees?

Is there a presentation you can give or a booklet you can leave them with, like Maker's Mark and Coldwell Banker? Is there some small reminder or totem you can create, like the Buffer sticker?

- Who would be on your internal brand task force? Remember, you want both worker bees and big thinkers.

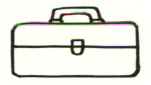

II

The Brand
NOW
Toolbox

Welcome to the Brand Now Toolbox!

Now that you understand the seven Brand Now Dynamics, it's time to put the system to work. This toolbox contains several concise tool chapters designed to help you implement the dynamics for different types of brands or in specific situations. There are also useful frameworks and diagrams to help you map your brand experience.

Every brand is different. Feel free to read this section in any order. Find an interesting topic and jump in. Like the trusty toolbox on your workbench, I hope you'll use this resource often in building your brand.

What's in the Brand Now Toolbox:

- → Brand Now: A Summary
- → Humor: The BONUS Eighth Dynamic
- → Brand Now for B2B Brands
- → Brand Now for Small-Business Brands
- → Brand Now for Personal Brands
- → Brand Now for Political Brands
- → Brand Now Naming
- → Brand Now Crisis Communication
- → Touchpoint Checklist
- → Touchpoint Map

P.S.: Be sure to check BrandNowBook.com for additional tools. If you have ideas for Brand Now tools you'd like to see, send them to me at nick@westergaard.com.

Summary

In putting the Brand Now Dynamics to work, a summary is a great place to start. This can also serve as a handy reference for revisiting these core concepts and sharing with others. First, there's a short summary. At 140 characters, it would make an ideal tweet. This is followed by a chapter-by-chapter breakdown of the seven dynamics.

Twitter Summary
Digital has changed branding but it still matters. To #BrandNow you need meaning, structure, story, content, community, clarity & experience.

Introduction
- Technology has changed the world around us—how we obtain information and make decisions about what to buy and what to support.
- While traditional brand advertising in the form of logos and 30-second ads isn't as powerful as it once was, brand-building still matters.
- To build brands, we need to embrace pattern recognition. To build a brand that stands out, we need to employ the seven dynamics of meaning, structure, story, content, community, clarity, and experience.

Chapter 1. Meaning

- In today's distracted digital world, people are looking for meaning more than ever.
- Understanding who your brand is, and what you stand for, starts with understanding your people. Go beyond the standard persona and develop a rich quantitative and qualitative customer profile to tease out what matters most to those you serve.
- To create meaning, you can appeal to your customers':
  - *Head*: Logical appeals like safety, flexibility, and simplicity.
  - *Heart*: Emotional appeals like belonging, style, and nostalgia.
- Historically, taking a stand socially and politically has been controversial. That's less and less the case. Don't be afraid to take bold stands as a brand if it aligns with your audience's core beliefs.

Chapter 2. Structure

- We're no longer branding at people, with logos and commercials. We are brand-building with our customers and communities.
- Brand DNA, as we understand it, has been re-sequenced. It's important for you to understand your brand's spark (why you're here) and promise (what you do and for whom).
- Think of your brand as a dimmer switch with dials that you can turn up and down for the various channels and touchpoints. Your job is to determine what is most important for your brand and, ultimately, those you serve.
- In some cases, you may turn the dimmer switches way down and be an alternative brand that stands out by what you choose *not* to do.
- Your brand is more than your logo, but visuals still matter. You can use visuals to reinforce the patterns of your brand.

Chapter 3. Story

- Stories are how we make sense of the world around us. Stories are patterns your brand can employ for communicating who you are and what you stand for.
- Vonnegut called them story shapes. Booker identified the seven plots that you can boil most stories down to, including overcoming the monster, rags to riches, the quest, voyage and return, and rebirth. You can employ archetypes in your brand story to trigger patterns your audience already has an understanding of.
- Other story principles that matter: The main character isn't you—it's your customer; conflict is good—it drives the story forward; and your brand has to have a distinct voice to stand out.

Chapter 4. Content

- The best way for moving your brand's story in today's distracted, digital world is with content. While this is a great tool . . .
- Caution: Everyone else knows this. That's why we're overwhelmed with content. Don't just create content because the other players in your industry do. Create content that's on brand—that conveys your meaning and tells your story as boldly as possible.
- Effective, standout content is both business-centric and customer-aware. Understand why you're creating this and who you're creating it for. Empathy is critical in creating customer-focused standout content.
- Create layers of content for various levels of customers: the skimmers, swimmers, and divers.

Chapter 5. Community

- When brands have meaning to the audience that they serve, people want to be a part of them. Belonging is one of the biggest needs out there.

- Get your arms around your brand's community by sorting them into concentric circles:
  - *Inner circle*: your employees.
  - *Middle circle*: vendors, partners, and anyone in between an employee and a customer.
  - *Outer circles*: your customers, starting with your best customers first. This is the inner circle of your outer circle. Your rabid fans are followed by your more transactional customers. Finally, you have your prospects and the general public.
- Start from the inside out. You should have a plan for engaging each group.

Chapter 6. Clarity

- Transparent, simple brands move faster than the opaque, complex alternatives.
- Transparency is a requirement when people have access to an unprecedented amount of information. There can be no disconnect between what your brand says and what it does.
- Simplicity is a powerful tool for communicating your brand's meaning and story. Improving your brand isn't always making it more complex. Look for areas where you can amplify by simplifying.

Chapter 7. Experience

- Experience is your brand promise delivered.
- Concentric circles can also guide you in mapping your brand's experience. Again, start with the inner circle and work outward (consult the map diagram at the end of this toolbox):

- *Core Brand DNA*: touchpoints include your spark, name, logo, brand promise, and core story.
- *Product/Service Experience*: touchpoints include your product or service itself, its packaging, and how it's taken to market (your website, your store, etc.).
- *Marketing/Communications Experience*: touchpoints here come in two categories—your static-analog touchpoints (broadcast media, direct mail, etc.), and interactive-digital touchpoints.

- Focus less on brand consistency (making sure everything looks the same) and more on brand coherence (making sure everything is saying the same thing, providing the same unifying meaning).
- One of the most powerful tools in building a standout brand is organizational culture. Look for ways to make your brand's meaning and story a part of the culture your employees are taught.

Humor:
The Bonus Dynamic

But wait—there's more! Yes, friends, there's an eighth bonus dynamic. And it's a funny one. I want to talk about how your brand can embrace humor. This wasn't rolled into the core seven because it's not as fully formed as those dynamics. That's not to say you couldn't flesh it out. Honestly, it could be a book unto itself. Instead, what I want to do is leave you with some key ideas on why humor matters for brands and how you can make it work for you and your brand.

Humor Cuts Through the Clutter and Delivers Meaning

Having a sense of humor baked into your brand can help you stand out exponentially. Nothing delivers connection and meaning faster than making someone laugh. A recent Nielsen study found that 47 percent of global respondents said that humorous ads resonated the most.[1]

For small, scrappy businesses and nonprofits, or those in notoriously dry industries (looking at you, my B2B friends), "humor can help you stand out in a crowded world," says Tim Washer, Creative Director at Cisco.[2] In this role, Washer produces hilarious videos for the B2B brand, including a popular video introducing a new server as the ideal Valentine's Day gift ("Nothing says I love you like six times the mobile backhaul capacity").[3]

In rolling out their mail-order razor/blade service, Dollar Shave Club needed to cut through the clutter of the billion-dollar shaving industry. They did so with a hilarious 90-second video tour of their innovative business by founder Michael Dubin, who proclaims at the outset: "Are the blades any good? No. Our blades are f**king great."[4]

What follows offers a mix of on-target product benefits (". . . each razor has stainless steel blades and an aloe vera soothing strip . . .") conveyed in a distinct brand voice ("Your handsome-ass grandfather had one blade. And polio.").[5] As always, the proof is in the pudding. Forty-eight hours after the video's debut on YouTube, Dollar Shave Club was laughing all the way to the bank with 12,000 people signed up for their service.[6]

There's no limit to who can use humor. You aren't bound by size, industry, budget, or any other constraint. That said, many still find excuses—even some of those just listed—for why they can't let their hair down and laugh a little. *That's not who we are. That's not the tone of our industry. We couldn't do that.* Too bad, because you're missing out.

So, how do you get started?

Surround Yourself with the Right People

If you think about it, Tim Washer's job title is something of an anomaly for a B2B brand like Cisco. But the forward-thinking company acknowledged that they could use someone whose work experience also includes *Saturday Night Live, Conan, The Onion,* and *Last Week Tonight with John Oliver.*

Most comedy starts in the writer's room, whether it's on a sketch show like *Saturday Night Live* or at a business like BarkBox. When you're a brand that goes for it with a meme such as Hump Day and much of your day is spent captioning dog photos, you clearly know how to bring the funny. But BarkBox Head of Content Stacie Grissom doesn't describe herself as funny. "I don't find myself to be the funniest person in the room. But because of that, I've only hired people on my team who are genuinely funny," says Grissom. "Don't try too hard—humor is something that needs to come naturally. And if it doesn't come naturally to you—find someone to help you out."[7] Hiring for a sense of humor can help you in more ways than one.

You may be able create a role internally for someone with a professional background in comedy, as Cisco did with Tim Washer. Or maybe you can just hire people who make you laugh like BarkBox. If you can't find anyone, reach out to a local improv theatre or the theatre department at a nearby college for help workshopping your brand. Being funny is a scary challenge. Make it less so by surrounding yourself with funny people who can help you.

How to Tell Funny (Brand) Stories

More often than not, stories are a delivery system for humor. As such, many of the Brand Now story elements can be helpful in uncovering humorous opportunities for your brand.

- **Story shapes.** Like the archetypes explored earlier, comedy comes with a few standard story shapes. The examples are too numerous to list here but include juxtaposition (Cisco employed this frame by juxtaposing the warmth of Valentine's Day with the cool gift of a business server) and satire (planning software Kinaxis uses the format of a dating show to illustrate why they're a "perfect partner").

- **Character.** Your main character shouldn't be your brand—it should be your audience. In looking for a way to showcase client testimonials, Cisco once again turned to Tim Washer who took the frame of the "awkward restaurant waiter" and set up vignettes featuring Cisco clients—Chief Information Officers (CIOs) from brands such as Western Union and the Denver Broncos—in a restaurant getting questioned by a nosy waiter (deftly played by Washer himself). The customers were front and center. So were the challenges they faced. . . .

- **Conflict.** In the 1989 classic *Crimes and Misdemeanors*, a blowhard comedy producer brilliantly portrayed by Alan Alda says, "If it bends, it's funny; if it breaks, it's not funny."[8] Most comedy comes from pain. In many cases your customers are in pain and you can help them. Humor allows you to explore the pain by casting it in a comedic light, not making fun of your customers or their feelings but instead sending up the circumstances. We weren't just laughing *at* the "Where's the beef?" lady in the Wendy's ads. We were laughing *with* her at the sad state of the fast-food hamburger. Allstate went so far as to personify the conflict in their ads featuring the troublemaker "Mayhem" who makes viewers thankful that they're insured. Of course, the ads are hilarious, but this is a powerful strategy in a business like insurance where the conflict is intangible ("What would happen if. . .?").

- **Voice.** The one rule of branding and comedy is that it has to fit you. And one of the biggest tests is whether or not humor fits with your brand voice. With new brands, this is easier as humor can be present going out of the gate. The Dollar Shave Club video introduced not only their brand but their voice. For years, the Charmin brand embraced a family-friendly voice in talking about bathroom business. "We know that social is a very noisy space and requires a CPG brand to do something unexpected in order to break through," says Laura Dressman, communications manager at Charmin.[9] That's why they regularly use scatological puns and the hashtag #tweetfromtheseat to weigh in on current events and pop culture. It's funny and still on brand. "They do potty humor, but in a fun way I can share with my kids," says digital strategist and author Jason Falls. "And when I'm walking down the big white aisle, I look for Charmin. Why? Because they make me laugh on the internet!"[10]

Many of these examples are humorous videos, but that's not the only place where you can use comedy. Old Spice has one of the more distinctive brand voices on social media, including irreverent tweets such as "You can tell a man's character by the firmness of his handshake, the Old Spice smell in his armpits, and how he punches robot alien invaders." The brand has even gone so far as to humorously engage with other brands such as Taco Bell.

Nineteenth-century actor Edmund Kean allegedly said, "Dying is easy. Comedy is hard." This rings especially true for brands, who by nature overthink even the most basic communication. That said, the payoff in both meaning and standing out to your audience is huge. "I don't think there's any brand that shouldn't be funny," says Eric Munn of Onion Labs, the content-services division of the venerable comedy publication *The Onion*, which works with brands like Audi, Bacardi, and Overstock to create engaging and humorous content on their platforms.[11]

Surround yourself with funny people and use the tools of storytelling—archetypes, characters, conflict, and voice—to find a way of embracing humor that fits for your brand. Go forth and be funny!

And don't forget to tip your wait staff.

P.S.: Many of the examples presented in this chapter are sight gags. Head over to BrandNowBook.com to view the videos referenced here.

Brand Now
for B2B Brands

These next few tools offer concise applications of Brand Now for specific types of brands. To be clear, I think that any brand, of any type, and in any industry, can embrace the seven dynamics along with humor. However, in my experience there are a few big categories of brands that face unique challenges and think of themselves very differently. I want to spend the next few pages not necessarily recasting the system laid out but rather spotlighting a few dynamics that can be of particular use.

Let's start with B2B brands.

The B2B Challenge

Nick, this (talk, book) had a lot of really nice ideas but, you see (*big pause*)—we're a B2B brand. *So . . . what*? Well, we have a very complicated product and we're in a very conservative industry. We can't do any of that. Plus our customers don't think of us like that. We're kind of a boring brand. (Nervous laugh.) This conversation—which I've had many times—doesn't contain reasons why you are unable to take a more progressive stance on brand-building. These are excuses for why you haven't done so yet.

Branding is bigger than ever in the B2B sector. During the past decade, B2B brands such as IBM and Oracle have dominated the Interbrand 100 list of top brands, increasing their share 42 percent year-on-year.[1] In fact, there are a few dynamics that work better because you're a B2B brand.

Meaning

That complicated product that you sell to a very particular customer? These "hurdles" can be tremendous assets. You know your customer even better than your B2C colleagues. Think of the customer target for Dollar Shave Club. Dudes (and ladies) who shave. Would you rather start with that blank page and a bunch of guesswork, or would you prefer a detailed profile of a very particular type of customer? The need that you're meeting is very specific. You can exploit this to develop a standout spark and promise for your brand. What you may have to do is dig a little deeper. For example, if you sell compliance software to financial service institutions, ask yourself what pain your product alleviates for your customer. Does your compliance software quell their regulatory fears? Does it make them feel safe and secure? That's meaning in both the head and the heart that you can build a brand on.

Structure

Remember the dimmer switches for choosing which structural elements you need to emphasize for your brand? With a prescriptive, complex sales cycle, you know which channels are most important and when. You know exactly which switches you can leave off. But don't forget about the power of alternative brands—doing what others aren't doing. Because B2B markets can be boring, it's easy to stand out by doing something that others aren't. While most B2B marketers would keep the dimmer turned way down on social bookmarking site Pinterest, email marketing software provider Constant Contact uses visual content on the network to engage their small business-owner clients. Their boards on the network feature "Monday Motivations" and "Quotes from Small Business Owners."

Content and Community

It's this same complex sales cycle that you can use to your advantage, creating content and keeping your audience engaged. In analyzing the various stages of your sales funnel, you can create content—webinars, ebooks, videos, and more—to help move them from one stage to the next. And a step closer to being your customer. Look for disruptions in the process. Where are they falling short? Use this as a content opportunity. Once they've purchased, some B2B brands bemoan that, in some cases, customers might not be in the market again for years. Use this as an opportunity to build an engaged community. What content could you offer your community after the sale? How can your brand be of use to them in their day-to-day lives moving forward?

Clarity

B2B brands are notoriously complicated. How can you stand out by subtracting? Simplifying has to count double in the overly complex B2B space! Inbound marketing platform Hubspot specializes in helping marketers navigate complex sales cycles. And they do it in a decidedly simple way—communicating the various areas of business they support through their "Growth Stack" consisting of CRM, Marketing, and Sales.

Humor

And, because juxtaposition is one of the most effective story archetypes found in comedy, humor can be a valuable tool in helping you stand out. You have a boring product in a boring industry? Have some fun with it, like Cisco's Valentine's Day server gift. "So much humor comes from pain," says Tim Washer. "We need to look for pain points that our customers have, and look for ways to create stories around solving them."[2] If your business really is dry, your customers probably know it, too. A well-timed laugh can put both parties at ease, building a strong, emotional connection between you and your customers. Who would you rather complete a lead form for: a brand that offered you an antiseptic post that you stopped reading, or a brand that made you laugh out loud?

Referencing a classic *Seinfeld* episode, Jason A. Miller, Global Content Marketing Leader at LinkedIn, calls this the George Costanza School of Branding. "Whatever they expect—do the opposite!"[3] That's why comedy can be such a welcome addition to the often buttoned-down world of B2B branding.

Brand Now
for Small Business Brands

Readers of *Get Scrappy* know that I have a special spot in my heart for small outfits trying to do more with less. Because small businesses are limited by resources, they, too, are often operating under the mistaken assumption that branding is a luxury that only big businesses can afford. If anything, the opposite is true. With half of small businesses closing their doors within five years of launching, your only chance of competing is to develop a standout brand.

The best part? In many cases, small entrepreneurial businesses are better equipped to develop bold brands. The reason? Fewer employees means fewer committees, which, in turn, means fewer obstacles to overcome. Small businesses are nimble and more willing to take risks.

While a small business brand can benefit from using the entire system, here are a few dynamics to focus your limited resources on. As my home state of Iowa is small and scrappy, it's no surprise that we're home to many small scrappy businesses as well. I've chosen a few of my favorites to bring these dynamics to life in a small business context.

Meaning

While many organizations struggle in search of meaning, small businesses often have this key piece of brand DNA readily available. Or, at the very least, you know where to find it. That's because in many cases the founder—the person who had that initial brand spark—is still roaming around the business. It's in these settings that you can have the history and purpose passed down to you like tribal knowledge.

Scratch Cupcakery is a four-location cupcake shop founded by Natalie Brown in Cedar Falls, Iowa. "Scratch was born from a love of making people smile. Since I was little, I've loved to bake for other people—creating recipes and sharing my ideas and experiments with anyone who would try," says Brown. Walk into Scratch and you'll see custom cupcakes like Banana Beer Walnut and Cap'n Crunch that are sure to bring a smile to your face. As any employee and their website home page will tell you, they're here to "make people smile—one cupcake at a time."[1]

If you don't know your small business's meaning, make time to talk with your founder right now.

Story

Interviewing the founder not only helps you unlock the meaning of your small business brand. It helps you put a spotlight on your story. For the discerning cheeseburger lover (read: *me!*), not all burgers are created equally. Short's Burger and Shine, in the heart of downtown Iowa City, is home to some of the most innovative cheeseburgers in the state such as the Thornton (chorizo, guacamole, mozzarella cheese, and chipotle mayo) and the PopeJoy (capocollo ham, provolone cheese, and muffuletta sauce).

The local food movement is at the heart of the Short's story. But instead of a "local" stamp in the corner of the menu, Short's devotes a whole paragraph and tells a real story:

Short's beef has not traveled far. Only 26.5 miles, to be exact. Our beef comes straight up Highway 218 from Ed Smith Farms, just north of Columbus Junction. Ed has been in the cattle business for over three decades, and raises the very best 100 percent cornfed beef. Bud's Meats in Riverside processes the beef and it arrives fresh, never frozen. Our buns are locally baked, and when in season, we purchase many vegetables from the farmer's market, Frytown produce and auction, and other local sources.[2]

Think back to the story archetype of The Quest. The protagonist sets out to acquire an important object, facing obstacles along the way. Short's story is a quest for the best local ingredients. The obstacles? Tempting frozen fast food from mysterious and faraway places. Short's wants to keep it in the community. Speaking of which . . .

Community

Community can be a powerful benefit for small business brands looking to do more with less. Remember to work your concentric circles—employees, partners, and customers (starting with your best customers and working your way out to your transactional customers). Some brands are literally built from the community. Mike Draper started selling quirky T-shirts on streets and college campuses before opening RAYGUN in downtown Des Moines's East Village. What started with the challenge of creating "ultra-positive" T-shirts about Des Moines grew into one of the Midwest's sassiest brands, with shirts featuring signature sayings such as "IOWA: 75% Vowels, 100% Awesome" and "Des Moines: Hell Yes." (Of course, my personal favorite is the quote of fictional Iowan Captain James T. Kirk, "No, I'm from Iowa. I only *work* in outer space.")

RAYGUN starts with their center circle of employees who help develop the snarky statements the company emblazons on shirts, magnets, and coasters. "It's a group effort," says Draper. "We have collaborative software where they can suggest ideas."[3] And, of course, the RAYGUN brand focuses on the communities they serve throughout the Midwest. "It's a heavy lift to build a brand; you really have to slowly build your customer base. We kind of like these more underrated Midwestern cities," adds Draper, who now also has RAYGUN shops in Cedar Rapids, Iowa City, and Kansas City.[4]

Another Iowa small business brand that takes care of their core customers is Luxe Interiors. The Coralville interior design boutique specializes in high-fashion home furnishings. But they recognize that most people aren't buying a couch every month. That's why they developed a program to keep their best customers close. The monthly Luxe Wine Club brings their community together for tastings, conversations, and fun. It also helps owner Jan Finlayson get to know their best customers even better. And, in the end, someone may see an end table or piece of art that they wouldn't have known about otherwise. This community-building strategy provides a good segue to another dynamic that small businesses can embrace—experience.

Experience

The size of a small business is also an advantage when it comes to experience. Because your business is smaller, you can exert greater control over all your brand touchpoints for a more coherent experience. Hills Bank and Trust Company, a bank with locations throughout eastern Iowa, does this with every brand touchpoint— from ATM receipts to their online videos. However, its headquarters in the small town of Hills, Iowa (population 806), offers the greatest expression of their brand experience.

Down the hall from the bank lobby you'll find a sign outside a door that simply states "History Room." Once you walk inside, the modern decor disappears as you're transported back to the brick walls of 1904—the year of the bank's founding. On those walls, you'll find a burglar alarm that used to hang outside the bank (fortunately, it was never needed, a sign notes), vintage banknotes, pens, and promotional items, and a sea of historic photos. To walk into this room is to walk into the brand's history. The Hills Bank History Room is the SPAM museum, small-business style.

In *Get Scrappy* I encourage readers to see ideas everywhere. Think of the last remarkable brand experience you had. How could you adapt this to fit your small-business brand?

Brand Now
for Personal Brands

I am consistently amazed by how often I am asked whether or not I believe that personal branding is "a thing." As someone who mentors students, advises employees, and helps individuals whose sole branded entity is themselves, I can tell you assuredly that personal branding is, in fact, "a thing." Some might say it's your most important thing, like entrepreneur Gary Vaynerchuk, who says, "It's important to build a personal brand because it's the only thing you're going to have. You've got to be out there at some level."[1]

I'm not sure why this is so hard for people. Perhaps those who struggle with it are working from a dated understanding of branding. Maybe they think it implies that individuals should have logos, a uniform, and a 30-second spot crafted by an advertising agency. That is, of course, ridiculous. But individuals can employ the seven dynamics to create a personal brand that people want to connect with and be a part of. It can serve a variety of objectives from job-seeking and promotion to building a personal brand for commercial purposes, such as working as a performer or professional speaker.

In his *Fast Company* essay "A Brand Called You," management legend Tom Peters wrote: "It's time to take a lesson from the big brands, a lesson that's true for anyone who's interested in what it takes to stand out and prosper in the new world of work. All of us need to understand the importance of branding. We are CEOs of our own companies: Me Inc. To be in business today, our most important job is to be head marketer for the brand called You."[2]

While you can employ the entire system of seven, here are a few dynamics you can use to help your personal brand stand out.

Meaning

You don't need a logo or ads for your personal brand. But you do need to stand for something. What's at the heart of great commercial brands is also at the center of great personal brands— meaning. Amazon CEO and founder Jeff Bezos says, "Your brand is what people say about you when you're not in the room." Personal brands can use this mantra quite literally. What do you want to be known for? Is it "sass," like Chelsea Handler? Is it "honesty," like Tom Hanks? Is it being a "maverick," like Richard Branson? Is it "hustle," like Gary Vaynerchuk? What's your personal brand spark? Use this as a touchstone in everything that you do as a personal brand. From what you wear and how you carry yourself to what you post on social media.

Story

Personal brands have stories, too. In thinking of personal brands that have meaning to you, you probably know their story by heart. As such, we can employ our story shapes and archetypes here as well. Is it overcoming the monster, or rags to riches? One word of caution in employing a story frame someone else is using—make sure what you're saying is true to your brand voice. You shouldn't take on someone else's story, complete with their voice, visuals, and other touchpoints. It sounds funny, but I'm sure you've seen someone very much trying to be someone they're not.

One thing that can be useful is one of Jay Acunzo's extractions outlined in Chapter One. Is there a personal brand from outside your industry who embodies what you're trying to do? Try positioning yourself as the "(ASPIRATIONAL BRAND) of (YOUR CATEGORY)." For example, as I mentioned in the introduction, Mitch Matthews once called me "the Indiana Jones of branding and marketing." As being both an educator and practitioner is an important part of my brand, this became a key frame for my story.

It takes more work, but you can also be an alternative brand by turning most of your touchpoints down. Warren Buffett is a bold business visionary because he doesn't do anything other business celebrities do. He doesn't tweet or give live-streaming keynotes. He doesn't wear flashy clothing. He's not on *Shark Tank*. He lives in Omaha, drinks Cherry Coke, and is quietly one of the greatest business minds of our generation. It's this last part that personal brands need to keep in mind—you have to be authentic. You have to have the goods.

Community

In addition to borrowing story archetypes from celebrity brands, you could also learn a thing or two about how to cultivate a fan culture around your personal brand. In addition to being the Global Content Marketing Leader at LinkedIn, Jason Miller is an accomplished rock-and-roll photographer. He's masterfully built a personal brand that straddles the diverse fields of marketing and rock photography (check out his work at http://rocknrollcocktail. com/). With up-close-and-personal access to rock legends, Miller notes that musicians like Dave Grohl and Andrew W.K. have built great brands by being approachable and making their fans a part of their process.

And don't forget to work all your concentric circles. Celebrity brands famously have their "squad" of friends such as Taylor Swift, but they also have circles of close fans such as Lady Gaga's "Little Monsters." John Green, author of *The Fault in Our Stars*, uses Twitter, Tumblr, and YouTube to communicate directly with his fans, sharing insights and updates on projects.

Clarity

"You can't hide anything," says Vaynerchuk. "Your reputation online and in the new business world is pretty much the game, so you've got to be a good person."[3] It sounds simple, but it's the only way to build an authentic brand. Consider actor Bill Murray's brand. While he's dry and sarcastic on-screen, he's unexpectedly warm and authentic offscreen. Whether he's dropping in to kickball games in New York, bartending at South by Southwest (SXSW), performing karaoke with strangers, or showing up at an LA ice cream social, Bill wanders in and brings his trademark magic. Being authentic and unexpected can help your brand stand out.

Brand Now
for Political Brands

In preparing the tools for this section of the book, I was excited to include something political. Reading and watching politics is one of my favorite pastimes. My home state also has the privilege of hosting the first-in-the-nation Iowa caucus. Like my fellow Iowans, I take this role seriously. That's why I've had my ear talked off by Joe Biden in a Pizza Ranch in Manchester and why I saw Lamar Alexander play the piano at a Sheraton in West Des Moines. I've also had the privilege of working on a few political campaigns, from local ballot initiatives and council races to statehouse runs. The fast pace of political campaigns often provides a proving ground for new marketing and media ideas.

You'd think that one of the more popular applications of personal branding would be in politics. And yet if you talk to a politician about their brand, you get one of two things: Either "Here's my sign!" or "Sit down—here's my stump speech. . . ." While these are certainly key touchpoints in political campaigns, they are not the sum total of your political brand.

The Brand Now system can be employed here as well. First, if you skipped the piece on personal branding, flip back and catch up.

Everything here builds on that foundation, because political brands are personal brands first and foremost.

Now let's get political.

Meaning

At this point you've probably already discovered that, although I highlight different dynamics for each audience segment, meaning has been a part of all of them. I can't stress this enough. Meaning— your spark, your purpose—is what can unite a sign and stump speech behind a bigger idea. "Hope and change" unified Barack Obama's 2008 and 2012 presidential campaigns. In working on smaller campaigns, candidates and volunteers always bemoan their budget. *We can't do the cool things the national candidates do.* Many times you actually can, because what they're really doing is grounded in strategic messaging—focusing on one core idea and layering on other, related ideas from there.

This is especially critical when you're running in a crowded field of candidates. Having what you're all about distilled into a one-word answer can help you stand out.

Structure

In a focused arena like politics, the brand touchpoints can be pretty prescriptive. Signs, signs, and more signs. Maybe spice things up with a sticker or a pencil. This is a great time to think about your brand's dimmer switch. Are there switches others are using? If you had asked me if embroidered red baseball caps would play a role in a major presidential campaign, I would have said no way. The election of Donald Trump proved me wrong. Visuals are also patterns that can help you stand out in a sea of dark suits on both male and female candidates. Whether it's Paul Simon's bow ties or Madeleine Albright's unique pins, look for ways to create memorable patterns of your own.

Story

Stories, too, are especially important for political brands. When there are subtle policy differences, so much comes down to a candidate's personality and story. If someone knows who you are, what you stand for, and where you come from, they'll feel a stronger connection to you. Take a moment and think of major politicians in modern history. We know their stories. We know Barack Obama's "rags-to-riches" story, growing up with a single mother in Hawaii and Indonesia (if you think about it, it's a perfect story for a candidate who's all about hope). We know about Ronald Reagan's background as an actor, his rise as governor of California, and eventually president (again, a Hollywood story that fits his "morning in America" message). We know Elizabeth Warren's professorial story. And we know Marco Rubio's family's immigrant story.

Successful politicians have stories that everyone knows. This is not a coincidence. Know your story. Tell it often. And don't forget . . .

Clarity

It goes without saying that political brands need clarity. First, in relation to meaning and storytelling, politicians need simplicity. If you get a candidate talking long enough, you can usually unearth both their big idea and their core story. What gets in the way is also simple—it's the candidate. If there's a field where the "more is better" fallacy is alive and well, it's politics. "If I have one minute for an answer, by God, I'll talk for two and half minutes until that poor moderator stops me!" But did you really say anything? When you have a concise, simple answer, people will remember it.

When you ramble, you get in the way of reinforcing your meaning. What's Bernie Sanders about? Financial-sector reform and income inequality. It's almost all he talks about. But there's no mistaking what he stands for, because Bernie has clarity. The same goes for stories. Don't obfuscate. "I was born poor and my father held down two jobs to send us to college, and that's why I want to make sure everyone has those same opportunities. . . ." In that sentence, I understand who you are and what you stand for.

And then there's transparency. Most will groan and say, "All politicians are liars." Sure, there are certainly elevated levels of exaggeration, but brands should be aspirational. That flag you plant and strive toward.

Humor

Politics is another field where you can stand out by employing humor. Like B2B marketers, this seems risky. Especially when the messaging from everyone else is grounded in gravitas. Don't forget that when you make someone smile, you endear yourself to them by connecting with them at an emotional level. You let some of the air out of the balloon.

That's what Gerald Daugherty did in Travis County, Texas. As a candidate for county commissioner, Daugherty had a lot of bright ideas on how to solve the community's problems, from taxes to public transportation. Instead of ads detailing his proposals, Daugherty's campaign created a video of him droning on and on around the house, while grilling with friends, during dinner, and while doing laundry. "Gerald really doesn't have any hobbies," his wife, Charlyn, grimly reports. "All he wants to do is fix things. Please re-elect Gerald. Please," she repeats in a perfect deadpan to the camera.[1] The voters of Travis County did just that.

Like Daugherty, to employ humor as a political brand, you—the candidate—have to be the brunt of the joke. But if you show you can laugh at yourself, you have a powerful tool for telling a standout story for your political brand. Plus, if you're a politician who can make people laugh (in a good way), you've got a leg up on the competition.

Brand Now Naming

Shakespeare's Juliet once asked, "What's in a name?" Um . . . kind of a lot, Jules. Choose wisely. Without a doubt, the single most important brand touchpoint is your name. If you're a personal or political brand, you're lucky. You already have a brand name. And in most organizations, in many cases, you've inherited a brand name. But if you're in a position to name a new brand, rename an existing brand, or develop a brand extension, then you have a daunting task ahead.

That's because a brand name has to do a lot. "It has to work emotionally, and it has to work rationally," says Mike Pile, president and creative director of Uppercase Branding, a verbal identity firm that specializes in creating powerful and evocative brand names for B2B clients such as Nokia, General Electric, FedEx, and others.[1] Properly constructed, a good brand name distills everything about your organization, product, or service into a few short words. Or, if you're *really* good, a single word.

Don't get scared, but naming is one of the biggest decisions you will make in the course of brand development. You should labor over it. You should have spirited debate. So, how do you get started? Once again, you can apply the Brand Now Dynamics in service of this complex task.

Meaning

Think back to your spark. Why are you here? What is the emotional result of the customer's experience with your brand? If this sounds "touchy-feely," consider the following. "A good name repositions the competition," says Marc Hershon, senior manager of naming and verbal identity in the San Francisco office of Landor. During his time at Lexicon Branding, he helped create memorable brand names such as BlackBerry, Swiffer, and Dasani.[2] When the BlackBerry came along, everything else in the space—such as the PalmPilot—had a literal name. The BlackBerry stood out as a composite tool with a composite name.

Mike Pile's tip for naming: Ask yourself this simple question—if your brand was a superhero, who would it be and why?[3] If your answer was The Flash, then speed is a part of what you do. If your answer was Captain America, then values are at your core. This is a great tool for overcoming obstacles in the creative process and getting at your brand's true essence.

Structure

Your brand name is a keystone to all other structural elements in your brand. But there's also structure involved in naming. Two popular structures for organizing your brand's naming platform are the branded house and the house of brands, Mike Pile shared.[4]

In some cases, you use a branded house such as Ford—with the Ford Explorer, Ford Escape, and so on (all have Ford at the beginning). In other situations, you go with a house-of-brands model such as P&G, which is made up of strong brands like Tide and Crest. Others still find a hybrid model effective, such as Hilton, which has both stand-alone brands like Hampton Inn and extensions like the Hilton Garden Inn. Even if you're developing a single brand name, keep structure and potential future scaling in mind.

Story

Your brand name should tell a story. Consider Tesla. This savvy bit of brand naming by founder Martin Eberhard anchored their start-up brand by honoring the legacy of Nikola Tesla, the Serbian-American genius who invented the AC induction motor, which the company planned on using in their electric car. They built their story by co-opting Nikola Tesla's story! As Marc Hershon notes, with strong brands "you have to be able to tell the story behind the name."[5]

Content

Your brand name will be a part of your content, whether it's expressly mentioned or simply the brand under which your content is released. While this isn't the most critical dynamic, it's one that merits consideration. Will people want to consume content that comes from this brand? You should also keep in mind the idea of creating a content brand as discussed in Chapter Four.

Community

Community is an invaluable and often-untapped asset in naming. Involve your people in your creative process. Assemble a casual meeting of team members from different areas who have an understanding of the brand you're trying to name. Don't necessarily ask them for naming ideas. Ask them what the product or service does, how it works, and how it benefits people. Your job is to take vigorous notes (it might be helpful to have someone transcribe what people are saying while you facilitate the conversation). If appropriate, host a similar meeting with a small group of customers or constituents.

When you're done, comb through your notes and identify common themes and keywords. Try combining some of the words.

When your brand name is rooted in words that your community is already saying, it will be easier for them to use it in conversations of their own. This should be a goal for any brand name.

Clarity

Transparency and simplicity are paramount in naming. Your name should be transparent, reflecting what you do and how you do it. That's not to say that it has to be literal. It could be transparent in conjuring up a mood. Tasty, Buzzfeed's comfort-food video series, is a great name because it paints a picture of the audience's emotional response. It's also simple. While naming requires coming up with lots of ideas, don't miss valuable insights from others in the room. During the pitch meeting for what would become the BlackBerry, someone on the team marveled that the small black pager with a tiny QWERTY keyboard "looked like a blackberry."[6]

In 2011, I was brought in to help President Obama's Council on Jobs and Competitiveness brand a job-skills training program for the manufacturing sector, which was—at that time—called the National Manufacturing Jobs Skills Accelerator. My first question was "Can we change the name?" We could, I was told, but I'd need to have a replacement the following week. Urgency led to clarity. *What does this program do? It ensures that job seekers have the right skills for the right jobs at the right time.* What about Right Skills Now? It was immediately adopted. The name had clarity and was also easily embraced in conversation by the community. In fact, the president even used the phrase during the State of the Union address.

Experience

Like content, this dynamic isn't as critical, but it's worth thinking about. You need to create a brand name with the rest of your experience in mind. How will your name be a part of your various touchpoints, both online and off?

And finally, here's my "lightning round" of additional brand-naming tips.

Additional Considerations

While there's no single formula for creating the perfect brand name, there are many common attributes that successful brand names have. A strong brand name is:

- **Unique**—Duh.
- **Easy to pronounce, spell, and memorize.** Clarity. This is a point many miss. Don't worry about coming up with the next Google, Yahoo!, or Zazzle. Aim for the next Groupon or HomeAway—descriptive and categorical, and, most important of all, easy to learn.
- **Evocative of your product/service/company benefits.** Like all marketing, start with the benefits, with the actual impact on your customers or the marketplace.
- **Suggestive to the product/service category.** Think of brands like BarkBox. Based on the name alone, the prospective customer has a general idea of what the company does. What does a made-up name like Altria tell you about what the company does? Also of note . . .
- **Real-world brand names are recalled at a higher rate.** Dawn Lerman of Fordham University and Ellen Garbarino of Case Western Reserve University found that real-word brand names are much more likely to be recalled than "nonword" brand names (68.8 percent recall versus 38.1 percent).[7]
- **Hard-to-recall names can be aided by a higher media spend for a teaching campaign.** But why wouldn't you build the strongest brand name going out of the gate and aim for higher recall? In an

era of rethinking how we spend money on paid media, we should work harder on the front end to create names that have legs of their own to travel virally.

And, of course, you want a name that is . . .

- **Trademarkable.** Use the U.S. Patent and Trademark Office's Trademark Electronic Search System (TESS) to conduct a quick trademark search.
- **Aligned with an available .com or .org domain name.** Unless you are really married to a concept, I advise steering clear of .net, .biz, etc. These are harder to recall than the more ubiquitous domain options. You'll want to keep your favorite domain registrar open in a tab as you search and get creative.
- **Usable on social media.** Along with domain availability, you have to consider character limits on social networks like Twitter and Instagram. Also, is the name available as a username on most popular networks?
- **Don't forget to Google your brand name idea.** Even if someone doesn't own the domain or have a trademark established, you could find someone on the web squatting on your concept or something very close to it. It pays to learn what's out there in advance.

A name is a cornerstone of your brand development. It will be a big hook that the marketplace will use to hang values upon. Give this touchpoint the time and attention it deserves.

Brand Now
Crisis Communication

The title of this tool was almost "When Bad Things Happen to Good Brands." But the truth is, when something bad happens—a crisis, a PR nightmare, a customer-service kerfuffle—and you've built a solid brand, you already have one thing working in your favor.

It's called "brand equity" for a reason. That's because the brand you've worked hard to create has real worth and value. Both tangible economic worth as an asset to your organization, and intangible emotional value in the hearts and minds of your community. In short, when you screw up, provided you're responsive and take ownership of the situation, your stakeholders are less likely to hold it against you.

However, just as you don't want to draw down your financial reserves, be careful not to burn up too much of this goodwill. In times of crisis, you can reinforce your standout brand by returning to some of the Brand Now Dynamics.

Meaning

Meaning is at the very heart of brand equity. If you stand for something, you mean something to your customers. This can be helpful when you're in a jam. While Tylenol's brand is built around pain relief, health underlies everything. This was tested in 1982, when a few of their bottles were laced with cyanide. Corporate parent Johnson & Johnson didn't miss a beat, issuing an enormous recall for 31 million bottles.[1] Their market share took a hit in the short term but rebounded within a year, due to their decisive actions in the face of this crisis. Their brand—who they are and what they stand for—served as a divining rod, leading them to the right response, right away.

In case of emergency... return to your brand's spark and promise. Who are you? What do you stand for? How does this latest crisis look when viewed through the lens of your brand's meaning? In communicating with your customers, consider reinforcing this.

Story

If story is how we make sense of the world on a good day, we lean on it even more so during a crisis. What's happening? What do we do now? Your customers need these answers, and so does your team. And they need them rapidly. The biggest shift in storytelling in the midst of a crisis is speed. "Things can get very emotional—and very impactful—very fast," says crisis communication expert Melissa Agnes, president and cofounder of Agnes+Day. "We have to be ready for that, and that's not easy. It involves a lot of education."[2] Because of this, it's important to have your core story distilled—its shape, your characters, and your brand voice—so that when it's called into action, you're ready.

JetBlue is on a quest to restore humanity to airline travel through innovations they pioneered, such as seatback entertainment and inflight yoga and Pilates instructions. In 2007, a massive ice storm crippled the airline's flights, creating countless delays and a customer-service nightmare. JetBlue founder David Neeleman responded with humanity and humility in a video, which he opened by addressing "My dear JetBlue customers."[3] He went on to reinforce their story, their brand promise, how they fell short, and what they would do differently in the future. And he did all this with a sincere voice and tone.

In case of emergency . . . revisit your core story and/or your story shape or archetype. How does the hero overcome obstacles? Can you employ some of these tools in the story of your response? Remember, time is of the essence. Failing to respond—or failing to respond in a timely manner—tells your customers a story as well.

Content

The JetBlue response also reminds us of the important role that content plays in times of crisis. The airline responded across many fronts. First was Neeleman's video with a personal apology and a promise. The airline was also an early adopter of social media for customer service. Once a crisis is over, many discontinue their crisis-response content. Not JetBlue. They used this crisis as an opportunity to create one of their most important pieces of content—their Customer Bill of Rights.

Created in the wake of one of their greatest customer-service challenges, this online document (https://www.jetblue.com/flying-on-jetblue/customer-protection/) starts by reinforcing their meaning: "JetBlue Airways is dedicated to inspiring humanity. We strive to make every part of your experience as simple and as pleasant as possible." It then continues with a very tactical set of expectations on scenarios such as cancellations, delays, and overbooking.[4] What started as a crisis response resulted in one of the most critical JetBlue brand touchpoints.

In case of emergency . . . how can you bring your response story to life for your customers through content? Remember, if the crisis is bad enough, you may need to repurpose your message across multiple content formats such as video, blog posts, and social media.

Community

Your community can also be an important asset in the middle of a crisis. If you create response content, they can help you share it. Sometimes they can even be your early warning system. Like when Maker's Mark decided that the only way they could answer growing customer demand was by reducing the proof of the spirit. They communicated this to members of their brand ambassador program first and were met with immediate resistance. "It took Coke nine months to see what they did [with New Coke]," says Maker's Mark Chairman Emeritus Bill Samuels Jr. "We knew in two days." They took immediate steps to reverse their decision, restoring the spirit to the delight of their fans.[5]

In case of emergency . . . remember to work your concentric circles of community as you communicate your response. Start with your raving fans, brand ambassadors, and other key customers. These loyal followers are more inclined to help you out, and, as Maker's Mark found, they often aren't afraid to tell you if you're screwing up.

Clarity

Transparency in what you say and what you do is a minimum requirement for organizations today. During an emergency, transparency is a no-brainer. You have to be clear in your response. This can be challenging if transparency hasn't previously been a part of your organizational culture. Clarity and transparency is another investment you can draw upon in times of crisis.

But simplicity is also required. When he first became director of the Hayden Planetarium at the American Museum of Natural History in New York, astrophysicist and author Neil deGrasse Tyson had trouble with his early media coverage. Specifically, he didn't like the sound bites the news chose from his expansive, scientific answers. "So I said, rather than have them sound-bite me, why don't I hand them sound bites that they can't edit. So I stood there in front of a mirror and I just barked out Saturn, black hole, big bang . . . and for every one of those words I said, 'What are three sentences I can put together, that are informative, make you smile, and are so tasty, you might want to tell someone else.'"[6] Using Tyson's tactics, you, too, can employ simplicity in sound-biting your crisis-response statements.

In case of emergency . . . both aspects of clarity can help you during challenging times. Transparency is required in all communications today, especially in the middle of an emergency. But you can't just employ this tactic on the day something goes wrong. You have to create a culture of transparency that goes all the way to the top of your organization. If this sounds hard now, it will be even harder in the midst of a crisis. Simplicity can also be your friend. More focus in your crisis communications ensures that your response is understood without other extraneous sound bites getting in the way.

Touchpoint Checklist

As discussed, your brand is made up of several touchpoints. Here is a checklist you can use to audit and align your brand touchpoints with the Brand Now Dynamics. You may also get an idea for a new touchpoint or two. You can also use this in conjunction with the brand touchpoint map that follows (used in Chapter Seven for mapping brand experience).

Core Brand DNA

- ❑ Name
- ❑ Logo
- ❑ Brand promise (mission statement, campaign tagline, etc.)
- ❑ Business cards
- ❑ Stationery
- ❑ Electronic templates—Word and PowerPoint
- ❑ Product design and packaging

Marketing Communications

- [ ] Advertising—digital (search, social, display), print, radio, television, and outdoor
- [ ] Brochures and collateral
- [ ] Direct mail
- [ ] Customer support—phone, email, text, social, in-person

Physical (Offline)

- [ ] Signage
- [ ] Interior design
- [ ] Employee uniforms and name tags
- [ ] Display screens
- [ ] Order forms
- [ ] Receipts
- [ ] Vehicles
- [ ] Trade-show and exhibit materials
- [ ] Promotional items and giveaways

Interactive (Online)

- [ ] Website
- [ ] Social media—both social profile artwork and the content posted there
- [ ] Content marketing—blog posts, social graphics, videos, podcasts, ebooks, white papers, case studies, infographics, and more
- [ ] Email marketing
- [ ] Employee email signatures

Additional

- ☐ Sensory—additional sounds, smells, etc.
- ☐ Employee orientation and organizational culture materials—onboarding and training programs

Touchpoint Map

Chapter Seven explored all the touchpoints that make up your brand experience. It also presented a process for mapping your brand touchpoints using concentric circles. Here you'll find a blank brand touchpoint map all ready for you to use. Enjoy!

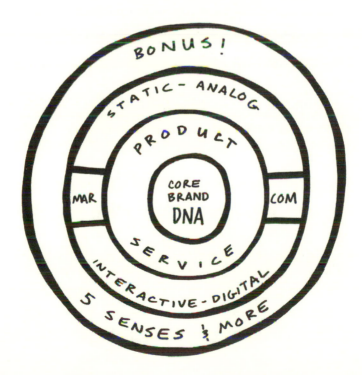

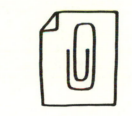

Appendix

Discussion Group Questions

If you read *Brand Now* with your team at work, in a classroom, or in a book group, here are some questions to spark follow-up discussions on the seven dynamics presented in the first part of this book.

Introduction

- What were some early brands that stood out to you in life? What made them special?
- How has branding changed since then?
- Think of the Interbrand four stages of branding—identity, value, experience, you. Can you think of some examples of each?
- What challenges concern you most about brand-building in the digital age?

Chapter 1. Meaning

- Think of one of your favorite brands. What do you think their spark is? What is their purpose?
- Do you think you might be an ideal customer persona for certain brands? Which ones?

- Based on this, how do those brands create meaning for you?

- Which brands have taken a stand socially or politically? Do you think it helped or hurt them?

Chapter 2. Structure

- Which brand touchpoints are most important today?

- Conversely, which touchpoints matter the least to you?

- Think back to the idea of the dimmer switch. Are there touchpoints you can turn up and others you can turn down?

- Who are some of your favorite alternative brands?

Chapter 3. Story

- What is an example of a story you've heard that moved you?

- List three of your favorite books or movies. Using the story archetypes presented, what common plots drive these stories?

- What is your brand's core story?

- Who is a brand that has a distinct voice? What characteristics embody this brand voice?

Chapter 4. Content

- What's an example of branded content that helped you out as a consumer?

- What type of content moves you the most? Blog posts? Videos? Podcasts? Something else?

- As there's too much content in the world, could you consider cutting your content quantity and focusing on your content quality? Can you think of other brands that have done this?

Chapter 5. Community

- Describe a way that you've seen a brand engage their community. Did they share customers' user-generated content? Did they tell their employees' stories? How did they make their people a part of their brand?

- Are there brands that have engaged people at all levels of the concentric circles described in Chapter Five—employees, partners, and customers?

- Have you ever encountered a brand ambassador for a company? If so, what was the ambassador program like?

Chapter 6. Clarity

- Think of a brand you know that was transparent. How did this transparency make you feel?

- Could you do something like this? What obstacles stand in your way?

- Who are your favorite simple brands? The ones who make it easy for you?

- Where can you simplify your brand? Can you amplify by subtracting?

Chapter 7. Experience

- Describe the most remarkable brand experience you've been a part of recently. It could be as small as opening a package or as big as visiting a special place such as the SPAM Museum or LEGOLAND. What made it so remarkable?

- Name a brand that has a powerful, coherent experience across all of their touchpoints.

- Have you observed a brand that has a strong culture internally? What stood out and why?

Further Reading and Resources

Looking for more great resources on the ideas laid out in *Brand Now*? Here are some of my favorites. All are books unless otherwise noted. I've tried to include parenthetical notes on where you can source videos and podcasts. For more links related to the stories in this book, check out the resources at BrandNowBook.com.

More on Meaning

- → *Predictably Irrational* by Dan Ariely
- → *Positioning* by Al Ries and Jack Trout
- → *Delivering Happiness* by Tony Hsieh
- → *The Red Thread*—video series from Tamsen Webster (tamsenwebster.com)

More on Structure

- → *The Brand Flip* by Marty Neumeier
- → *Primal Branding* by Patrick Hanlon
- → Marc Shillum: *Consistent Brands Through Repeating Patterns*—Video (Vimeo)

More on Story

→ *Story* by Robert McKee
→ *The Seven Basic Plots* by Christopher Booker
→ *The Business of Story*—Podcast hosted by Park Howell (businessofstory.com)
→ Andrew Stanton: *The Clues to a Great Story*—TED Talk (YouTube)
→ Kurt Vonnegut on *Story Shapes*—Video (YouTube)

More on Content

→ *Everybody Writes* by Ann Handley
→ *They Ask, You Answer* by Marcus Sheridan
→ *The Story of Content*—Documentary film by the Content Marketing Institute (YouTube)

More on Community

→ *Think Like a Rockstar* by Mack Collier
→ *Zappos Culture Book*—https://www.zapposinsights.com/culture-book
→ *Beyond the Brick:* A LEGO Brickumentary—Documentary film (iTunes)

More on Clarity

→ *The Responsible Company* by Yvon Chouinard and Vincent Stanley
→ *The Naked Brand*—Documentary film (iTunes)
→ *Global Brand Simplicity Index*—Annual study by Siegel+Gale (http://simplicityindex.com/)

More on Experience

→ *What Great Brands Do* by Denise Lee Yohn

→ *What Customers Crave* by Nicholas J. Webb

More on Humor

→ *Truth in Comedy* by Del Close, Charna Halpern, and Kim "Howard" Johnson

→ To view the humorous brand videos referenced in the toolbox chapter, head over to BrandNowBook.com

More on Personal Branding

→ *Known* by Mark W. Schaefer

→ *Reinventing You* by Dorie Clark

→ *The Road to Recognition* by Seth Price and Barry Feldman

→ "A Brand Called You" by Tom Peters, Fast Company article at https://www.fastcompany.com/28905/brand-called-you

More on Political Branding

→ View Texas County Commissioner Gerald Daugherty's humorous ad at BrandNowBook.com

More on Naming

→ For links to the naming resources referenced in the toolbox chapter, go to BrandNowBook.com

More on Crisis Communication

→   Crisis expert Melissa Agnes's website is home to many helpful resources including flowcharts, infographics, and the *Crisis Intelligence* Podcast (http://melissaagnes.com/)

→   For links referenced in this toolbox chapter, including video of Neil deGrasse Tyson talking about sound bites, head over to BrandNowBook.com

Acknowledgments

Concentric circles were a big theme in *Brand Now*. I'd be nothing without my own circles of community, especially when faced with the task of writing a book.

Speaking at events feeds my soul. Many of the ideas found here were born from talks with marketers and brand-builders at conferences and corporate events throughout the world. Ironically, *Get Scrappy* originated from a talk at MarketingProfs's annual B2B Forum. It's only fitting that the first place I uttered the phrase *Brand Now* was at their event in 2015.

I'm grateful to the team at AMACOM for believing in me once again. Their editorial insight, careful production, and dedication are unparalleled in publishing. More than an editor, Ellen Kadin's ideas often lead to game-changing edits in structure and style. Bradley Dicharry is a talented graphic designer and longtime friend who communicates my vision when my drawings fall short. And none of this would be possible without Giles Anderson, a standout literary agent. He often understands what I'm trying to say before I do. I'm fortunate to have you all as partners in this process.

Speaking of professionals, I'm thankful to my work communities at Brand Driven Digital and the University of Iowa's Tippie College of Business. From helping clients to interviewing podcast guests to teaching students, everything I say and write is built on this foundation. Thanks to my work teams at both, especially Andrea Luangrath in the marketing department at Tippie, who pointed me to several helpful studies.

Sometimes standout brands are hiding in plain sight. Luckily, my community of Facebook friends served as informal research assistants, guiding me to great brands doing interesting things. Thanks to Tim Andersen, Jennifer Angerer, Katya Boltanova, Christy Bonfig, Holly Bonfig Becker, Chris Brogan, Sheryl Brown-Madjlessi, Mike Carberry, Clint Carroll, Andrew B. Clark, Taylor Corrigan, Dave Cutler, Fabio Dall'Oglio Cunha, Jackson Doran, Staci Drew, Lisa Du Bois Low, Paul Dunckel, Jon Engelhardt, Jason Falls, Brian Fanzo, Dan Farkas, Mike Finlayson, Gordon Fischer, Kurt Michael Friese, Mike Gerholdt, Jeff Hamlett, Jess Harris, Tim Hayden, Rob Hill, Jennifer Horn Frasier, Mitch Joel, Melissa KH, Jason Keath, Doug Kessler, Kelly Kingman-Joslyn, Bryan Kramer, Christina Kroemer, John LaBella, Rachelle Lucas, Rod McCrea, Forrest Meyer, Scott Monty, Chris Moody, Amber Naslund, Sheila Ongie, Amber Osborne, Kerry O'Shea Gorgone, Lonny Pulkrabek, Shuva Rahim, Danielle Rogers, Robert Rose, Blake Rupe, Angelika Schwaff, Pamela Slim, Tom Slockett, Daniel Smith, Seth Sparks, Eric Swayne, Tim Washer, Tamsen Webster, Tom Webster, Harry Westergaard, Molly Wilson, Ted Wilson, and Rob Zaleski.

Special thanks also to my close collaborators Ann Handley, Gini Dietrich, and Rob Rouwenhorst. What an *Oceans 11*–like expert heist team I assembled! Ann is a writer's writer, Gini is a master of grammar, style, and wit, and Rob, as always, double-checked both my research and my Star Trek references. Each read the manuscript with care, offering input, suggestions, and feedback that made the book you're reading immeasurably better.

Finally, my family—my inner circle. Thanks to Harry, Sam, Adrien, Mia, and Jude. From Costco to the SPAM Museum, our adventures together inspire me constantly. I love watching you all discover the world. And lastly, the innermost circle, partner in life, work, and all endeavors—thank you, Meghann. A standout among standouts.

Notes

Introduction

1. Albee, Edward. *The Zoo Story*, Samuel French, 1959.
2. "The Four Ages of Branding," Interbrand, accessed July 17, 2017, http://interbrand.com/views/the-four-ages-of-branding/.
3. The CMO Survey, *The CMO Survey* (North Carolina, Fuqua School of Business, Duke University/Deloitte/American Marketing Association, 2017).
4. Ibid.
5. "dynamic." Dictionary.com, accessed July 17, 2017, http://www.dictionary.com/browse/dynamic.
6. Gabor, Deb. Interview by Nick Westergaard, *On Brand* (podcast), Brand Driven Digital, August 22, 2016, http://www.branddriven digital.com/brand-yourself-or-you-risk-being-branded-by-others/.

Chapter 1: Meaning

1. Parkhurst, Emily. "In most cities, Starbucks is a neighborhood bellwether. In Seattle, not so much," *Puget Sound Business Journal*, March 5, 2015.
2. *The Princess Bride*. Dir. Rob Reiner. Perfs. Mandy Patinkin, Wallace Shawn. 20th Century Fox, 1987. DVD.
3. "logos." An Intermediate Greek-English Lexicon, accessed July 17, 2017, http://www.perseus.tufts.edu/hopper/text?doc=Perseu%3A text%3A1999.04.0058%3Aentry%3Dlo%2Fgos.
4. Frankl, Victor. *Man's Search for Meaning* (Boston: Beacon Press, 1946, 2006).
5. "5 Gaps Between Brand Strategy Theory And Practice," Branding Strategy Insider, accessed July 17, 2017, https://www.branding strategyinsider.com/2016/06/10675.html#.WW0KbdPyvx5.

6. Di Somma, Mark. Interview by Nick Westergaard, *On Brand* (podcast), Brand Driven Digital, January 11, 2016, http://www .branddrivendigital.com/understanding-brand-strategy-with-mark-di-somma/.

7. "meaning." Dictionary.com, accessed July 17, 2017, http://www .dictionary.com/browse/meaning.

8. "Chip Wilson, Lululemon Guru, Is Moving On," *New York Times Magazine*, accessed February 17, 2017, https://www.nytimes .com/2015/02/08/magazine/lululemons-guru-is-moving-on .html?_r=2.

9. "They'll Spoil Your Dog Every Month," *New York Magazine*, accessed July 17, 2017, http://nymag.com/shopping/features/ barkbox-2012-5/.

10. "Inside Amazon's Idea Machine: How Bezos Decodes Customers," *Forbes*, accessed July 17, 2017, https://www.forbes.com/sites/ georgeanders/2012/04/04/inside-amazon/#44d9083e6199.

11. Morgan, John Michael. Interview by Nick Westergaard, *On Brand* (podcast), Brand Driven Digital, March 21, 2016, http://www .branddrivendigital.com/everything-you-do-is-branding-john-michael-morgan/.

12. Yohn, Denise Lee. *What Great Brands Do* (San Francisco: Josey-Bass, 2014).

13. Norton, Michael I., Daniel Mochon, and Dan Ariely. "The IKEA effect: When labor leads to love," *Journal of Consumer Psychology* 22 (2012), 453–460.

14. Acunzo, Jay. Interview by Nick Westergaard, *On Brand* (podcast), Brand Driven Digital, January 9, 2017, http://www.branddriven digital.com/moving-brand-average-exceptional-jay-acunzo/.

15. Joachimsthaler, Erich. Interview by Nick Westergaard, *On Brand* (podcast), Brand Driven Digital, November 7, 2016, http://www .branddrivendigital.com/impact-social-currency-branding-erich-joachimsthaler/.

16. Johnson, Carla. Interview by Nick Westergaard, *On Brand* (podcast), Brand Driven Digital, January 16, 2017, http://www .branddrivendigital.com/creating-stories-from-customer-empathy-with-carla-johnson/.

17. "No more smokes at CVS," CNN Money, accessed July 17, 2017, http://money.cnn.com/2014/09/03/news/companies/cvs-cigarettes/index.html.

18. "About Luvvie Ajayi," Luvvie.org, accessed July 17, 2017, http:// luvvie.org/about/.

19. "Coke ran an old diversity-themed commercial before the Super Bowl, and people are mad," Mashable, accessed July 17, 2017, http://mashable.com/2017/02/05/super-bowl-coke-ad-mad/#xYo_wuWvHmqw.

20. Howell, Park. Interview by Nick Westergaard, *On Brand* (podcast), Brand Driven Digital, July 27, 2015, http://www.branddrivendigital.com/how-to-tell-your-brand-story-with-park-howell/.

Chapter 2: Structure

1. Pink, Daniel H. *To Sell Is Human* (New York: Riverhead Books, 2012).

2. Nielsen, JA, BA Zielinski, MA Ferguson, JE Lainhart, JS Anderson. "An Evaluation of the Left-Brain vs. Right-Brain Hypothesis with Resting State Functional Connectivity Magnetic Resonance Imaging," PLoS ONE 8(8): e71275. https://doi.org/10.1371/journal.pone.0071275 (2013).

3. "Tesla Generates Small Sales, Big Buzz Without Paid Ads," *Advertising Age*, accessed July 17, 2017, http://adage.com/article/news/tesla-generates-small-sales-big-buzz-paid-ads/241994/.

4. Ibid.

5. "Elon Musk (@elonmusk) | Twitter," Twitter.com, accessed July 17, 2017, https://twitter.com/elonmusk.

6. "BuzzFeed's Foodie Channels Are Blowing Up on Facebook," *Fortune*, accessed July 17, 2017, http://fortune.com/2016/01/19/buzzfeed-tasty-proper-tasty/.

7. Kozinets, Robert V. "Can Consumers Escape the Market? Emancipatory Illuminations from Burning Man," *Journal of Consumer Research, Inc.,* Vol. 29, June 2002.

8. Whitson JA, AD Galinsky, "Lacking control increases illusory pattern perception," *Science*, Oct 2008: Vol. 322, Issue 5898, pp. 115-117, DOI: 10.1126/science.1159845.

9. "Branding Is About Creating Patterns, Not Repeating Messages," Fast Co. Design, accessed July 17, 2017, https://www.fastcodesign.com/90127471/we-studied-brands-around-the-world-what-consumers-want-isnt-what-you-think.

10. Ibid.

Chapter 3: Story

1. "Storynomics: How to Create a Story That Inspires with Robert McKee," *Convince and Convert,* accessed July 17, 2017, http://www.convinceandconvert.com/podcasts/episodes/storynomics-how-to-create-a-story-that-inspires/.

2. "A creative writing lesson from the 'God of Story'," *Guardian*, accessed on July 17, 2017, https://www.theguardian.com/books/2016/sep/10/creative-writing-lesson-god-of-story-robert-mckee-tim-lott.

3. "The Science of Storytelling: What Listening to a Story Does to Our Brains," Buffer, accessed on July 17, 2017, https://blog.buffer-app.com/science-of-storytelling-why-telling-a-story-is-the-most-powerful-way-to-activate-our-brains.

4. "Nancy Duarte: How to Tell a Story," Stanford Graduate School of Business–YouTube, accessed July 17, 2017, https://www.youtube.com/watch?v=9JrRQ1oQWQk.

5. "The science of the story," University of California-Berkeley, accessed on July 17, 2017, http://news.berkeley.edu/berkeley_blog/the-science-of-the-story/.

6. "Kurt Vonnegut graphed the world's most popular stories," *Washington Post*, accessed on July 17, 2017, https://www.washingtonpost.com/news/wonk/wp/2015/02/09/kurt-vonnegut-graphed-the-worlds-most-popular-stories/?utm_term=.e1b47628e878.

7. Booker, Christopher. *The Seven Basic Plots* (New York: Continuum, 2004).

8. "DollarShaveClub.com - Our Blades Are F***ing Great," DollarShaveClub.com–YouTube, accessed July 17, 2017, https://www.youtube.com/watch?v=ZUG9qYTJMsI.

9. Grant, Adam. *Originals* (New York: Penguin, 2016), 134–135.

10. Neumeier, Marty. *The Brand Flip* (San Francisco: Peachpit Press, 2016).

11. Webster, Tamsen. Interview by Nick Westergaard, *On Brand* (podcast), Brand Driven Digital, January 1, 2015, http://www.branddriven digital.com/beyond-the-positioning-statement-with-tamsen-webster/.

12. Lehew, Bobby. Interview by Nick Westergaard, *On Brand* (podcast), Brand Driven Digital, November 23, 2015, http://www.brand drivendigital.com/how-brands-can-tell-better-stories-with-bobby-lehew/.

13. Handley, Ann (author of *Everybody Writes* and *Content Rules*), in discussion with the author, July 2017.

14. "Duluth Trading Company History," Duluth Trading Company, accessed July 17, 2017, https://www.duluthtrading.com/features/DuluthHistory.aspx.

15. Duluth Trading Company Catalog, Vol. M17, No. 06, April 2017.

16. "HENRIK WERDELIN: BarkBox & Prehype," Phase:3, accessed July 17, 2017, http://www.phase3mc.com/on-branding/episode-036-henrik-werdelin-barkbox-prehype/.

17. Grimm, Lisa. Interview by Nick Westergaard, *On Brand* (podcast), Brand Driven Digital, April 25, 2016, http://www.branddriven digital.com/behind-the-scenes-of-the-whole-foods-brand-voice/.

18. Brand & Voice, Uberflip Brand & Style Guide, accessed July 17, 2017, https://styleguide.uberflip.com/uberflip-brand-style-guide/.brand-voice.

19. Batiz, Suzy. Interview by Nick Westergaard, *On Brand* (podcast), Brand Driven Digital, March 28, 2016, http://www.branddriven digital.com/poopourri-uses-humor-to-humanize/.

20. Ibid.

21. Ibid.

22. "Mars rover Curiosity takes to Twitter to tell the 'inside' story," NBC News, accessed July 17, 2017, http://www.nbcnews.com/id/48493172/ns/technology_and_science-space/t/mars-rover-curiosity-takes-twitter-tell-inside-story/#.WW0jodPyvx5.

23. Green, Richard. *Te Ata: Chickasaw Storyteller, American Treasure* (Oklahoma: University of Oklahoma Press), 19.

Chapter 4: Content

1. "GoPro: Hovercraft Deer Rescue," GoPro–YouTube, accessed July 18, 2017, https://www.youtube.com/watch?v=cgnceHH_p_I.

2. "Eric Schmidt: Every 2 Days We Create As Much Information As We Did Up To 2003," Techcrunch, accessed July 27, 2015, http://techcrunch.com/2010/08/04/schmidt-data.

3. "Annual Research: Content Marketing Budgets, Benchmarks and Trends," Content Marketing Institute, accessed July 18, 2017, http://contentmarketinginstitute.com/research/.

4. Ibid.

5. Schaefer, Mark W. *The Content Code* (Louisville: Grow Publishing, 2015).

6. "Annual Research: Content Marketing Budgets, Benchmarks and Trends," Content Marketing Institute, accessed July 18, 2017, http://contentmarketinginstitute.com/research/.

7. Johnson, Carla. Interview by Nick Westergaard, *On Brand* (podcast), Brand Driven Digital, January 16, 2017, http://www.branddriven digital.com/creating-stories-from-customer-empathy-with-carla-johnson/.

8. Ibid.
9. Sheridan, Marcus. Interview by Nick Westergaard, *On Brand* (podcast), Brand Driven Digital, February 6, 2017, http://www.brand drivendigital.com/answering-customers-questions-marcus-sheridan/.
10. Davis, Andrew. Interview by Nick Westergaard, *On Brand* (podcast), Brand Driven Digital, January 12, 2015, http://www.branddriven digital.com/why-content-brands-trump-branded-content-with-andrew-davis/.
11. Pulizzi, Joe. Interview by Nick Westergaard, *On Brand* (podcast), Brand Driven Digital, September 7, 2015, http://www.brand drivendigital.com/why-brand-constraints-inspire-creativity-with-joe-pulizzi/.
12. "BlendTec–YouTube Channel," YouTube, accessed July 18, 2017, https://www.youtube.com/user/Blendtec.
13. Kessler, Doug. Interview by Nick Westergaard, *On Brand* (podcast), Brand Driven Digital, February 27, 2017, http://www.branddriven digital.com/aim-brand-content-marketing-win-doug-kessler/.
14. "CIA shares a bizarre Shark Week history lesson starring the Navy and Julia Child," *Washington Post*, accessed July 18, 2017, https://www.washingtonpost.com/news/checkpoint/wp/2015/07/10/cia-shares-a-bizarre-shark-week-history-lesson-starring-julia-child/?utm_term=.6dc7898c6101.
15. Handley, Ann. Interview by Nick Westergaard, *On Brand* (podcast), Brand Driven Digital, October 31, 2016, http://www.branddriven digital.com/brands-editor-chief-ann-handley/.
16. Ibid.
17. "Survey of 1000+ Bloggers: How to Be in the Top 5%," Orbit Media, accessed on July 18, 2017, https://www.orbitmedia.com/blog/blogger-analysis/.
18. Rose, Robert. Interview by Nick Westergaard, *On Brand* (podcast), Brand Driven Digital, December 12, 2016, http://www.brand drivendigital.com/brands-and-content-marketing-with-robert-rose/.
19. "Ira Glass–Here's The Thing–WNYC," WNYC, accessed July 18, 2017, http://www.wnyc.org/story/ira-glass-interview/.
20. Gerhardt, Dave. Interview by Nick Westergaard, *On Brand* (podcast), Brand Driven Digital, January 30, 2017, http://www.branddriven digital.com/standing-creating-content-customers-want-dave-gerhardt/.

Chapter 5: Community

1. "Enterprise: The First Space Shuttle," Mental Floss, accessed July 18, 2017, http://mentalfloss.com/article/28146/enterprise-first-space-shuttle.

2. "Why Employee Advocacy Can't Wait," LinkedIn Marketing Solutions Blog, accessed July 18, 2017, https://business.linkedin.com/marketing-solutions/blog/linkedin-elevate/2017/why-employee-advocacy-cant-wait.

3. Kaplan, Robert S., and David P. Norton. "The Office of Strategy Management," *Harvard Business Review*, October 2005.

4. Zappos.com, *2009 Culture Book* (Las Vegas: Zappos.com, Inc., 2009).

5. "Zappos CEO Tony Hsieh: full interview transcript," *Marketplace*, accessed July 18, 2017, https://www.marketplace.org/2010/08/19/business/corner-office/zappos-ceo-tony-hsieh-full-interview-transcript.

6. Li, Charlene, with Jon Cifuentes and Brian Solis, "Strengthening Employee Relationships in the Digital Era," Altimeter Group, December 16, 2014.

7. Blankenship, Sean. Interview by Nick Westergaard, *On Brand* (podcast), Brand Driven Digital, March 7, 2016, http://www.branddrivendigital.com/branding-at-coldwell-banker/.

8. Ibid.

9. Coldwell Banker, *Brand Storybook* (San Francisco: Coldwell Banker, 2016).

10. Slaski, Jen. Interview by Nick Westergaard, *On Brand* (podcast), Brand Driven Digital, June 13, 2016, http://www.branddrivendigital.com/creating-culture-brand-camp-spiceworks/.

11. Samuels, Jr., Bill. Interview by Nick Westergaard, *On Brand* (podcast), Brand Driven Digital, April 24, 2017, http://www.branddrivendigital.com/the-history-of-the-makers-mark-brand/.

12. Ibid.

13. Slaski, Jen. Interview by Nick Westergaard, *On Brand* (podcast), Brand Driven Digital, June 13, 2016, http://www.branddrivendigital.com/creating-culture-brand-camp-spiceworks/.

14. Zissimos, John. Interview by Nick Westergaard, *On Brand* (podcast), Brand Driven Digital, May 16, 2016, http://www.branddrivendigital.com/branding-at-salesforce/.

15. Zappos.com, *2009 Culture Book* (Las Vegas: Zappos.com, Inc., 2009).

16. LaCroix, Steve. Interview by Nick Westergaard, *On Brand* (podcast), Brand Driven Digital, December 14, 2015, http://www

.branddrivendigital.com/a-fan-engagement-lesson-from-the-minnesota-vikings/.

17. Slaski, Jen. Interview by Nick Westergaard, *On Brand* (podcast), Brand Driven Digital, June 13, 2016, http://www.branddriven digital.com/creating-culture-brand-camp-spiceworks/.

Chapter 6: Clarity

1. "clarity." Dictionary.com, accessed July 18, 2017, http://www.dictionary.com/browse/clarity.
2. Webster, Tamsen (Message Strategist), in discussion with the author, April 2017.
3. "United Breaks Guitars," Sons of Maxwell–YouTube, accessed July 18, 2017, https://www.youtube.com/watch?v=5YGc4zOqozo.
4. "2017 Edelman Trust Barometer," Edelman, accessed July 18, 2017, http://www.edelman.com/trust2017/.
5. "Nielsen: Global Consumers' Trust in 'Earned' Advertising Grows In Importance," Nielsen, accessed July 18, 2017, http://www.nielsen.com/us/en/press-room/2012/nielsen-global-consumers-trust-in-earned-advertising-grows.html.
6. Srere, David B. Interview by Nick Westergaard, *On Brand* (podcast), Brand Driven Digital, April 6, 2015, http://www.branddriven digital.com/branding-with-simplicity-at-siegelgale/.
7. "2017 Edelman Trust Barometer," Edelman, accessed July 18, 2017, http://www.edelman.com/trust2017/.
8. "2016 Transparency ROI Study," Label Insight, accessed July 18, 2017, https://www.labelinsight.com/Transparency-ROI-Study.
9. Ibid.
10. *The Naked Brand.* Dir. Jeff Rosenblum and Sheung-Lee Huang. Film Buff, 2013. DVD.
11. Ibid.
12. "Patagonia Mission Statement: Our Reason for Being," Patagonia.com, accessed July 18, 2017, http://www.patagonia.com/company-info.html.
13. *The Naked Brand.* Dir. Jeff Rosenblum and Sheung-Lee Huang. Film Buff, 2013. DVD.
14. Yohn, Denise Lee. *What Great Brands Do* (San Francisco: Josey-Bass, 2014).
15. "Just Add Sugar," *New Yorker*, accessed July 18, 2017, http://www.newyorker.com/magazine/2013/11/04/just-add-sugar.
16. "Chobani–Beliefs," Chobani, accessed on July 18, 2017, http://www.chobani.com/ethos.

17. "Global Brand Simplicity Index 2017," Siegel+Gale, accessed July 18, 2017, http://simplicityindex.com/.
18. Edison Research, *The Infinite Dial* (New Jersey, Edison Research/ Triton Digital, 2015).
19. *The Naked Brand*. Dir. Jeff Rosenblum and Sheung-Lee Huang. Film Buff, 2013. DVD.
20. Acunzo, Jay. Interview by Nick Westergaard, *On Brand* (podcast), Brand Driven Digital, January 9, 2017, http://www.branddriven digital.com/moving-brand-average-exceptional-jay-acunzo/.
21. Srere, David B. Interview by Nick Westergaard, *On Brand* (podcast), Brand Driven Digital, April 6, 2015, http://www.brand drivendigital.com/branding-with-simplicity-at-siegelgale/.

Chapter 7: Experience

1. "SPAM® Ingredients & History," SPAM® Brand, accessed July 19, 2017, http://www.spam.com/about.
2. Grissom, Stacie. Interview by Nick Westergaard, *On Brand* (podcast), Brand Driven Digital, April 18, 2017, http://www.branddriven digital.com/barkbox-branding-convergence-culture-audience/.
3. "Groundbreaking Study Shows Link Between Customer Experience and Stock Performance," Cision, accessed July 19, 2017, http:// www.prnewswire.com/news-releases/groundbreaking-study-shows-link-between-customer-experience-and-stock-performance-201223311.html.
4. "Almost all consumers abandon brands after one bad experience," CMO Innovation, accessed July 19, 2017, https://www .enterpriseinnovation.net/article/almost-all-consumers-abandon-brands-after-one-experience-247006285.
5. "Groundbreaking Study Shows Link Between Customer Experience and Stock Performance," Cision, accessed July 19, 2017, http://www.prnewswire.com/news-releases/groundbreaking-study-shows-link-between-customer-experience-and-stock-performance-201223311.html.
6. "Brands must match experience to marketing," Marketing Week, accessed July 19, 2017, https://www.marketingweek.com/2012/07/17/brands-must-match-experience-to-marketing/.
7. Srere, David B. Interview by Nick Westergaard, *On Brand* (podcast), Brand Driven Digital, April 6, 2015, http://www.branddriven digital.com/branding-with-simplicity-at-siegelgale/.
8. *To Kill a Mockingbird*. Dir. Robert Mulligan. Perfs. Gregory Peck, Mary Badham. Universal, 1962. DVD.

9. Jordan, Justine. Interview by Nick Westergaard, *On Brand* (podcast), Brand Driven Digital, September 28, 2015, http://www .branddrivendigital.com/designing-the-customer-experience-with-justine-jordan/.

10. "The smell of commerce: How companies use scents to sell their products," *The Independent,* accessed July 30, 2017, http://www .independent.co.uk/news/media/advertising/the-smell-of-commerce-how-companies-use-scents-to-sell-their-products-2338142.html.

11. Thurston, Baratunde. "Hot on the Paper Trail," *Fast Company,* March 17, 2014.

12. Yohn, Denise Lee. *What Great Brands Do* (San Francisco: Josey-Bass, 2014).

13. "coherent." Merriam-Webster, accessed July 28, 2017, https://www .merriam-webster.com/dictionary/coherent.

14. Sullivan, Barbara Apple. Interview by Nick Westergaard, *On Brand* (podcast), Brand Driven Digital, March 9, 2015, http://www .branddrivendigital.com/brand-consistency-vs-brand-coherence-with-barbara-apple-sullivan/.

15. Miles, Josh. Interview by Nick Westergaard, *On Brand* (podcast), Brand Driven Digital, August 3, 2015, http://www.branddriven digital.com/brand-unity-vs-uniformity-with-josh-miles/.

16. Ibid.

17. Batiz, Suzy. Interview by Nick Westergaard, *On Brand* (podcast), Brand Driven Digital, March 28, 2016, http://www.branddriven digital.com/poopourri-uses-humor-to-humanize/.

18. "Girls Don't Poop–PooPourri.com," YouTube, accessed July 19, 2017, https://www.youtube.com/watch?v=ZKLnhuzh9uY.

19. "Branding Is About Creating Patterns, Not Repeating Messages," Fast Co. Design, accessed July 17, 2017, https://www.fastcodesign .com/90127471/we-studied-brands-around-the-world-what-consumers-want-isnt-what-you-think.

20. Neumeier, Marty. *The Brand Flip* (San Francisco: Peachpit Press, 2016).

21. Grissom, Stacie. Interview by Nick Westergaard, *On Brand* (podcast), Brand Driven Digital, April 18, 2017, http://www.brand drivendigital.com/barkbox-branding-convergence-culture-audience/.

22. Samuels, Jr., Bill. Interview by Nick Westergaard, *On Brand* (podcast), Brand Driven Digital, April 24, 2017, http://www.brand drivendigital.com/the-history-of-the-makers-mark-brand/.

23. Batiz, Suzy. Interview by Nick Westergaard, *On Brand* (podcast), Brand Driven Digital, March 28, 2016, http://www.branddriven digital.com/poopourri-uses-humor-to-humanize/.

24. "Buffer security breach has been resolved—here is what you need to know," Buffer, accessed July 19, 2017, https://open.buffer.com/buffer-has-been-hacked-here-is-whats-going-on/.

25. McLellan, Drew. Interview by Nick Westergaard, *On Brand* (podcast), Brand Driven Digital, December 21, 2015, http://www.branddrivendigital.com/why-your-brand-should-be-aspirational-with-drew-mclellan/.

26. Wyatt, Thom. Interview by Nick Westergaard, *On Brand* (podcast), Brand Driven Digital, July 6, 2015, http://www.branddrivendigital.com/how-employee-engagement-builds-brands-with-thom-wyatt/.

27. McLellan, Drew. Interview by Nick Westergaard, *On Brand* (podcast), Brand Driven Digital, December 21, 2015, http://www.branddrivendigital.com/why-your-brand-should-be-aspirational-with-drew-mclellan/.

28. Ibid.

Humor: The Bonus Dynamic

1. "Digital Formats Are Among the Most Trusted Advertising Sources Despite Slow Growth," Nielsen, accessed July 19, 2017, http://www nielsen.com/us/en/insights/news/2015/digital-formats-are-among-the-most-trusted-advertising-sources-despite-slow-growth.html.

2. Washer, Tim. Interview by Nick Westergaard, *On Brand* (podcast), Brand Driven Digital, July 13, 2017, http://www.branddrivendigital.com/should-your-brand-try-comedy-ciscos-tim-washer-has-the-answer/.

3. "A Special Valentine's Day Gift . . . from Cisco!" YouTube, accessed July 19, 2017, https://www.youtube.com/watch?v=Z8M-Wl9UGwQo.

4. "DollarShaveClub.com - Our Blades Are F***ing Great," Dollar-ShaveClub.com – YouTube, accessed July 17, 2017, https://www.youtube.com/watch?v=ZUG9qYTJMsI.

5. Ibid.

6. "How a Dollar Shave Club's Ad Went Viral," *Entrepreneur*, accessed July 19, 2017, https://www.entrepreneur.com/article/224282.

7. Grissom, Stacie. Interview by Nick Westergaard, *On Brand* (podcast), Brand Driven Digital, April 18, 2017, http://www.branddriven digital.com/barkbox-branding-convergence-culture-audience/.

8. *Crimes and Misdemeanors.* Dir. Woody Allen. Perfs. Woody Allen, Alan Alda. Orion, 1989. DVD.

9. "The Choice of Voice: How Humor Helps Define Charmin's Brand," Marketing Tango, accessed July 19, 2017, http://www.marketing-tango.com/choice-voice-humor-helps-define-charmins-brand/.

10. Falls, Jason. Interview by Nick Westergaard, *On Brand* (podcast), Brand Driven Digital, May 9, 2016, http://www.branddrivendigital .com/brands-need-to-listen-up-says-elasticitys-jason-falls/.

11. Munn, Eric. Interview by Nick Westergaard, *On Brand* (podcast), Brand Driven Digital, February 15, 2016, http://www.branddriven digital.com/how-the-onion-helps-brands-bring-the-funny/.

Brand Now for B2B Brands

1. "Best Brands—Interbrand," Interbrand, accessed July 19, 2017, http://interbrand.com/best-brands/.

2. Washer, Tim. Interview by Nick Westergaard, *On Brand* (podcast), Brand Driven Digital, July 13, 2017, http://www.branddrivendigital .com/should-your-brand-try-comedy-ciscos-tim-washer-has-the-answer/.

3. Miller, Jason. Interview by Nick Westergaard, *On Brand* (podcast), Brand Driven Digital, March 16, 2015, http://www.branddriven digital.com/how-to-rock-your-brands-content-on-linkedin-with-jason-miller/.

Brand Now for Small Business Brands

1. "About Scratch Cupcakery," Scratch Cupcakery, accessed July 19, 2017, http://www.scratchcupcakery.com/about-us.

2. Menu from Short's Burger and Shine (Iowa City, Iowa: 2017).

3. "RAYGUN: An Iowa-born, Midwest-centric clothing company that thrives on being clever, quirky and kitschy," My Favorite Places, accessed July 19, 2017, http://www.myfaveplaces.com/ shop/2016/9/13/raygun-an-iowa-born-midwest-centric-clothing-company-that-thrives-on-being-clever-quirky-and-kitschy.

4. "#MaeveWest: See the T-shirts that are edgy—for Iowa," CNN, accessed July 19, 2017, http://www.cnn.com/2015/07/29/politics/ maevewest-raygun-des-moines-2016/index.html.

Brand Now for Personal Brands

1. "100+ Best Personal Brand Quotes Ever," Seth Price, accessed July 19, 2017, http://www.sethprice.net/personal-branding-quotes/.

2. Peters, Tom. "The Brand Called You," Fast Company, August 31, 1997.
3. "100+ Best Personal Brand Quotes Ever," Seth Price, accessed July 19, 2017, http://www.sethprice.net/personal-branding-quotes/.

Brand Now for Political Brands

1. "Gerald Daugherty Campaign: Please Re-Elect Gerald . . . Please!" YouTube, accessed July 19, 2017, https://www.youtube.com/watch?v=wzjRwNUQDRU.

Brand Now Naming

1. Pile, Mike. Interview by Nick Westergaard, *On Brand* (podcast), Brand Driven Digital, November 28, 2016, http://www.brand drivendigital.com/develop-right-brand-name-naming-expert-mike-pile/.
2. Hershon, Marc. Interview by Nick Westergaard, *On Brand* (podcast), Brand Driven Digital, May 11, 2015, http://www.branddrivendigital.com/how-to-create-a-brand-name-with-naming-expert-marc-hershon/.
3. Pile, Mike. Interview by Nick Westergaard, *On Brand* (podcast), Brand Driven Digital, November 28, 2016, http://www.branddriven digital.com/develop-right-brand-name-naming-expert-mike-pile/.
4. Ibid.
5. Hershon, Marc. Interview by Nick Westergaard, *On Brand* (podcast), Brand Driven Digital, May 11, 2015, http://www.branddrivendigital.com/how-to-create-a-brand-name-with-naming-expert-marc-hershon/.
6. Ibid.
7. Lerman, D., and E. Garbarino. "Recall and recognition of brand names: A comparison of word and nonword name types" (2002). Psychol. Mark., 19: 621–639. doi:10.1002/mar.10028.

Brand Now Crisis Communication

1. "How the Tylenol murders of 1982 changed the way we consume medication," PBS NewsHour, accessed July 19, 2017, http://www.pbs.org/newshour/updates/tylenol-murders-1982/.
2. Agnes, Melissa. Interview by Nick Westergaard, *On Brand* (podcast), Brand Driven Digital, October 24, 2016, http://www.branddrivendigital.com/creating-crisis-ready-brand-melissa-agnes/.

3. "Our promise to you," JetBlue–YouTube, accessed July 19, 2017, https://www.youtube.com/watch?v=-r_PIg7EAUw.
4. "JetBlue | Customer protection," JetBlue, accessed July 19, 2017, https://www.jetblue.com/flying-on-jetblue/customer-protection/.
5. Samuels, Jr., Bill. Interview by Nick Westergaard, *On Brand* (podcast), Brand Driven Digital, April 24, 2017, http://www.brand drivendigital.com/the-history-of-the-makers-mark-brand/.
6. "Neil deGrasse Tyson on the Anatomy of a Soundbite," American Museum of Natural History YouTube Channel, accessed July 19, 2017, https://www.youtube.com/watch?v=lLT1xpbTvZ.

Index

About the Author

NICK WESTERGAARD is a strategist, speaker, author, and educator. As Chief Brand Strategist at Brand Driven Digital, he helps build better brands at organizations of all sizes—from small businesses to Fortune 500 companies. Nick is the author of *Get Scrappy: Smarter Digital Marketing for Businesses Big and Small*.

He is a contributor to the *Harvard Business Review* and host of the popular *On Brand* podcast. His thoughts have been featured in news sources such as *US News & World Report*, *Entrepreneur*, *Forbes*, Mashable, and more.

Nick is a sought-after keynote speaker on branding and marketing at conferences and corporate events throughout the world. He also teaches at the University of Iowa, where he sits on the Advisory Council of the Marketing Institute at the Tippie College of Business and the Professional Advisory Board for the School of Journalism and Mass Communication. He is also a mentor at the Iowa Startup Accelerator.

Nick lives with his wife and five kids in Coralville, Iowa.

Find him online at nickwestergaard.com and @nickwestergaard on Twitter.